WRITER-FILES

General Editor: Simon Trussler

Associate Editor: Malcolm Page

File on
SHEPARD

Compiled by John Dugdale

Methuen Drama

A Methuen Drama Book

First published in 1989 as a paperback original
by Methuen Drama, Michelin House,
81 Fulham Road, London SW3 6RB
and HEB Inc., 70 Court Street, Portsmouth
New Hampshire 03801, USA

Copyright in the compilation
©1989 by John Dugdale
Copyright in the series format
©1989 by Methuen Drama
Copyright in the editorial presentation
©1989 by Simon Trussler

Typeset in 9/10 Times
by L. Anderson Typesetting
Woodchurch, Kent TN26 3TB

Printed in Great Britain by
Richard Clay Ltd, Bungay, Suffolk

British Library Cataloguing in Publication Data

Dugdale, John
    File on Shepard — (Writer-files)
    I. Title   II. Series
    822'.914

    ISBN 0-413-17410-7

Contents

The theatre is, by its nature, an ephemeral art: yet it is a daunting task to track down the newspaper reviews, or contemporary statements from the writer or his director, which are often all that remain to help us recreate some sense of what a particular production was like. This series is therefore intended to make readily available a selection of the comments that the critics made about the plays of leading modern dramatists at the time of their production — and to trace, too, the course of each writer's own views about his work and his world.

In addition to combining a uniquely convenient source of such elusive *documentation*, the 'Writer-Files' series also assembles the *information* necessary for readers to pursue further their interest in a particular writer or work. Variations in quantity between one writer's output and another, differences in temperament which make some readier than others to talk about their work, and the variety of critical response, all mean that the presentation and balance of material shifts between one volume and another: but we have tried to arrive at a format for the series which will nevertheless enable users of one volume readily to find their way around any other.

Section 1, 'A Brief Chronology', provides a quick conspective overview of each playwright's life and career. *Section 2* deals with the plays themselves, arranged chronologically in the order of their composition: information on first performances, major revivals, and publication is followed by a brief synopsis (for quick reference set in slightly larger, italic type), then by a representative selection of the critical response, and of the dramatist's own comments on the play and its theme.

Section 3 offers concise guidance to each writer's work in non-dramatic forms, while *Section 4*, 'The Writer on His Work', brings together comments from the playwright himself on more general matters of construction, opinion, and artistic development. Finally, *Section 5* provides a bibliographical guide to other primary and secondary sources of further reading, among which full details will be found of works cited elsewhere under short titles, and of collected editions of the plays — but not of individual titles, particulars of which will be found with the other factual data in Section 2.

The 'Writer-Files' hope by striking this kind of balance between information and a wide range of opinion to offer 'companions' to the study of major playwrights in the modern repertoire — not in that dangerous pre-digested fashion which can too readily quench the desire to read the plays themselves, nor so prescriptively as to allow any single line of approach to predominate, but rather to encourage readers to form their own judgements of the plays in a wide-ranging context.

Sam Shepard writes plays of imagistic detail with the broad brush-strokes of epic: specifically, the epic that has been spun around the American West, and which has become one of the tributary sources for what we glibly call the American dream — glibly, because, as Shepard's plays recognize, dreams have their roots not in the ostensibly rational impulse to succeed of the 'protestant work ethic', but in the fragmented and often tortured realms of the subconscious. He began writing, as he interestingly records on page 59 of this volume, from the 'outside in' — that is, from his perception of the 'shared emotional territories' in which his characters entrap themselves rather than from within their minds. And this was creatively daring in a nation obsessed with understanding itself from the 'inside out', whether on the analyst's couch or through the style that has become known as 'method' acting. But in words — as in the music (jazz, rock, country) which has so often been integral to his work — Shepard has nonetheless become the man who struck the lost chord of the American consciousness: and his plays reverberate tanta-lizingly in the mind, so close to a truth about their society, yet evading precise examination or definition, as the words and music create their elusive, almost vorticist synthesis of stage sounds and images.

Shepard writes on page 58 about the commercial and even artistic pressures against a playwright permitting a play to make its own length. Whether in response to such pressures or not, his later work has sometimes acquired a deceptively naturalistic gloss, as he has found himself permitting his characters a little more say in their theatrical circumstances — enmeshed as they now often are in that collective 'emotional territory' that is the family. Yet the stage world they inhabit remains curiously limited in its common denominators, and Shepard's characters are for ever scurrying back to their own interior landscapes. And so, as he himself puts it on page 58, the plays are 'always unfinished, always imagistic, having to do with recalling experiences through a certain kind of vision'. The critics in this volume try to pin down that vision too closely at their peril: it evades words, just as words are part of the evasion it embodies. Some argue that it is a vision so distinctively American that British actors find it difficult to render it wholly or with emotional truth: yet Shepard himself spent some time in Britain, and his plays have often been premiered here. Truly, 'the West' of which he writes is of the mind, whose 'language' knows no frontiers.

Simon Trussler

1943 5 November, born in Fort Sheridan, Illinois, as Samuel Shepard Rogers III (called 'Steve'). Eldest of three children of Sam Rogers, Sr., then a pilot, and Jane Elaine Rogers, a schoolteacher. Early childhood spent at different military bases, in South Dakota, Utah, Florida, and Guam.

1949 Starts school in South Pasadena, a suburb east of Los Angeles where the family lived after his father left the Army Air Corps.

1955 When 'eleven or twelve', family moves to avocado ranch with livestock in Duarte, California; his teenage years are spent here.

1960-61 Graduates from High School. Begins first of three semesters at Mount San Antonio Junior College, taking courses in education and agricultural science. First experiences of acting and writing.

1963 Arrives in New York after eight months as actor in theatre company touring North East. Lives on Lower East Side with Charles Mingus Jr., son of jazz musician, and works as waiter at Village Gate club in Greenwich Village.

1964 First plays, *Cowboys* and *Rock Garden,* performed in double bill, October.

1965-66 Escapes draft, on basis of supposed heroin addiction. Succession of rapidly composed one-act plays establishes his reputation as leading writer of new 'Off-Off-Broadway' theatre. First Obies (Off-Broadway awards) for *Chicago*, *Icarus's Mother*, and *Red Cross*.

1967 First two-act play, *La Turista,* and first productions of *Melodrama Play, Cowboys No. 2,* and *Forensic and the Navigators.*

1968-69 Continues to write for stage, but also travels to Europe to work on Antonioni's film *Zabriskie Point,* and (unproduced) Rolling Stones movie *Maxagasm.* Plays drums on album by the Holy Modal Rounders. Marries actress O-Lan Johnson, November 1969.

1970 *Operation Sidewinder* staged unsuccessfully at Lincoln

Center, New York, March — his largest cast and most ambitious Broadway production to date. Son Jesse Mojo born, May.

1971 Lives in London with O-Lan and Jesse. Originally intends to become rock musician, but writes *The Tooth of Crime*, *Geography of a Horse Dreamer*, and *Action*.

1972 *The Tooth of Crime* premiered at Open Space Theatre, London.

1973 *Blue Bitch* staged at Theatre Genesis, New York, and transmitted on BBC Television. *Hawk Moon* published.

1974 *Geography of a Horse Dreamer* and *Little Ocean* both premiered in London.

1975-76 After his return to California, becomes associated with Magic Theater in San Francisco, where many of his subsequent works receive their first productions. Tours New England with Bob Dylan's 'Rolling Thunder Revue', Fall 1975.

1977 *Curse of the Starving Class*, first 'country' play, staged, April. *Rolling Thunder Logbook* published.

1978 *Seduced, Tongues* (with Joseph Chaikin) and *Buried Child*, which wins Pulitzer Prize for Drama. First major film role in Terrence Malick's *Days of Heaven*.

1979 Second collaboration with Chaikin in *Savage/Love*.

1980 *True West* staged in San Francisco, July, and (after dispute) in New York, December. Shepard appears in the film *Resurrection*, with Ellen Burstyn.

1981 Appears in the film *Raggedy Man*, with Sissy Spacek. Also filming *Frances*, with Jessica Lange.

1982 *Motel Chronicles* published.

1983 *Fool for Love* staged, February. Appears as Chuck Yeager in Philip Kaufman's film *The Right Stuff*, and later receives Academy Award nomination as Best Supporting Actor.

1984 Release of *Paris, Texas*, dir. Wim Wenders, first complete screenplay to be filmed; wins Golden Palm for Best Film at Cannes

Festival. Appears with Jessica Lange in *Country*, and now living with her, initially in New Mexico. Death of Sam Rogers, Sr., March. Divorce from O-Lan Shepard, July.

1985   Directs first production of *A Lie of the Mind*, December. Stars in Robert Altman's film of *Fool for Love*, with Kim Basinger.

1986   Receives New York Drama Critics' Award for *A Lie of the Mind*. Appears in Bruce Beresford's film *Crimes of the Heart*.

1987   Appears in the film *Baby Boom*, starring Diane Keaton.

a: Stage Plays

For further bibliographical details of collections of plays cited,
see Section 5, 'Primary Sources'. References to *The Unseen
Hand and Other Plays* are to the 1986 edition unless otherwise
stated. References to *American Dreams* are to Bonnie
Marranca, ed., *American Dreams: the Imagination of Sam
Shepard* (New York: Performing Arts Journal Publications,
1981). References to 'Shepard, interview in *Theatre
Quarterly*' are to Sam Shepard, interviewed by Kenneth
Chubb and the Editors, 'Metaphors, Mad Dogs, and Old-Time
Cowboys', *Theatre Quarterly*, IV, No. 15 (1974), p. 3-16.

Cowboys

One-act play.
First production: Theatre Genesis at St. Marks Church-in-the-
Bowery, New York, Oct. 1964, in double bill with
The Rock Garden (dir. Ralph Cook).

*Two young men in an unidentified space act out their
fantasies: they try out various accents, wait for rain,
fight off an Indian attack, describe imaginary
breakfasts, avoid police sirens, practise baseball, and
finally turn on the audience.*

The playwright's name is Sam Shepard, and I know nothing
about him except that he has written a pair of provocative and
genuinely original plays ... working with an intuitive approach
to language and dramatic structure and moving into an area
between ritual and naturalism, where character transcends
psychology, fantasy breaks down literalism, and the patterns of
ordinariness have their own lives ... One comes away feeling
that the playwright has kept some of his secrets, perhaps kept
them from himself, but at least he has secrets to keep.
    Michael Smith, 'Theatre', *Village Voice*, 22 Oct. 1964, p. 13

The head-waiter at the Village Gate was a guy named Ralph Cook, and he had been given this church, called St. Mark's in the Bowery, and he started a theatre there called Theatre Genesis. He said he was looking for new plays to do, and I said I had one. He came up and he read this play, and two of the waiters at the Village Gate were the actors in it. So it was sort of the Village Gate company. Well, Jerry Talmer from the *Post* came, and all these guys said it was a bunch of shit, imitated Beckett or something like that. I was ready to pack it in and go back to California. Then Michael Smith from *Village Voice* came up with this rave review, and people started coming to see it.

Shepard, interview in *Theatre Quarterly*, p. 6

The Rock Garden

One-act play.
First production: in double bill with *Cowboys*, details as above. Final
   scene included in the 'erotic revue' *Oh! Calcutta!*, 1969.
*Published: Mad Dog Blues and Other Plays; The Unseen Hand and
   Other Plays.*

Rock Garden *is about leaving my mom and dad. It happens in two scenes. In the first scene the mother is lying in bed ill while the son is sitting in a chair, and she is talking about this special sort of cookie that she makes, which is marshmallow on salt crackers melted under the oven. It's called angels on horseback, and she has a monologue about it. And then the father arrives in the second scene. The boy doesn't say anything, he's just sitting in this chair, and the father starts to talk about painting the fence around the house, and there's a monologue about that in the course of which the boy keeps dropping asleep and falling off his chair. Finally the boy has a monologue about orgasm that goes on for a couple of pages and ends in him coming all over the place, and then the father falls off the chair. The father also talks about this rock garden, which is his obsession, a garden where he collects all these rocks from different sojourns to the desert.*

Shepard, interview in *Theatre Quarterly*, p. 8

11

Up to Thursday

One-act play.
First production: Playwrights Unit of Theater 1965 at Village South Th.,
    New York, 23 Nov. 1964.
Revived: in triple bill at Cherry Lane Th., New York, 10 Feb. 1965
    (dir. Charles Gyns).
Unpublished.

Up to Thursday *was a bad exercise in absurdity, I guess. This
kid is sleeping in an American flag ... and there's four people on
stage who keep shifting their legs, and talking.*

Shepard, as above

Dog

One-act play.
First production: La Mama ETC, New York, 10 Feb. 1965, in double
    bill with *Rocking Chair.*
Unpublished.

Dog *was about a black guy — which later I found out it was
uncool for a white to write about in America. It was about a
black guy on a park bench, a sort of* Zoo Story-*type play.*

Shepard, as above

Rocking Chair

First production: in double bill with *Dog*, details as above.
Unpublished.

I don't even remember Rocking Chair, *except it was about
somebody in a rocking chair.*

Shepard, as above

Chicago

One-act play.

First production: Theatre Genesis at St. Marks Church-in-the-
Bowery, New York, 16 Apr. 1965 (dir. Ralph Cook; with
Kevin O'Connor).

Revived: Cafe La Mama, 13 and 17 Mar. 1966; Martinique Th.,
12 Apr. 1966; La Mama European tour, 1967.

*Published: Five Plays; Chicago and Other Plays; The Unseen Hand
and Other Plays.*

---

*A fantasy comedy about a young man in a bathtub. ... As he sits
in his tub, singing, soliloquizing, following the darting of his
daydreams in rhyme, reason and unreason, we learn that the girl
who lives with him has got a job and is leaving that day. She
passes through several times. So do friends, who breakfast with
her before she goes ... this is a free-flowing, salty rhapsody on a
small incident seen through the prism of fancy.*

Stanley Kauffmann, *New York Times*, 13 Apr. 1966, p. 36

The disorientation contained in the presence of the bathtub — a real
object — on an empty stage rather than in a bathroom setting reflects
Stu's condition. He is an inert object stranded between two realities, his
fantasies and the world outside himself, trapped by an overwhelming
fear of activity. As Joy's vacation is enacted expressionistically, Stu
imagines her vacation to be the prelude to a mass suicide. Pushing these
fantasies to excess, Shepard means to overwhelm the audience with the
existential fear that, in our alienating environment, makes even simple
activities difficult.

Michael Bloom, 'Visions of the End',
in *American Dreams*, p. 74

4-H Club

One-act play.

First production: Playwrights Unit at Cherry Lane Th., New York,
Sept. 1965 (dir. Charles Gyns).

Published: The Unseen Hand and Other Plays.

13

Three young men in a trash-filled apartment: with occasional outbreaks of violence and shouting, they talk about making coffee, sweeping up, apples, lawns, and mice.

Icarus's Mother

One-act play.
First production: Caffe Cino, New York, 16 Nov. 1965 (dir. Michael Smith).
First London production: Open Space Th., Spring 1971 (dir. David Benedictus).
Published: Five Plays; The Unseen Hand and Other Plays.

Five young people watch a plane flying overhead, after finishing a Fourth of July barbecue. They talk about the pilot, and look forward to the evening's firework display. Eventually, the two girls return from a walk reporting that the jet flew low over the beach and crashed; one of the men, in a final monologue punctuated by firework sounds, evokes its fall into the sea.

I was in Wisconsin, in Milwaukee, and for the Fourth of July we have this celebration — fireworks and all that kind of stuff — and I was in this sort of park with these people, with this display going on. You begin to have a feeling of this historical thing being played out in contemporary terms — I didn't even know what the Fourth of July meant, really, but here was this celebration taking place, with explosions. One of the weird things about being in America now, you don't have any connection with the past, with what history means: so you can be there celebrating the Fourth of July, but all you know is that things are exploding in the sky. And then you've got this emotional thing that goes a long way back, which creates a certain kind of chaos, a kind of terror ...

Shepard, interview in *Theatre Quarterly*, p. 9

Up until now ... what Shepard's plays are about is a great deal less interesting than how they are about it. ... I suspect that [*Icarus's Mother*] is very much about something, but it is Shepard's way that if we have to ask ourselves what it is, then it becomes nothing. ... If Shepard is beginning to superimpose message, or symbol, or story, or, indeed, naturalistic motivation on the existing, very great 'reality' of his plays, he must start taking into account the very different artistic responsibilities these usually very normal elements impose on him.

Edward Albee, 'Theatre',
Village Voice, 25 Nov. 1965, p. 19

Red Cross

One-act play.
First production: Judson Poets' Th., New York, 20 Jan. 1966
(dir. Jacques Levy, with Lee Kissman, Joyce Aaron).
Revived: Provincetown Playhouse in double bill, 28 Apr. 1968.
First London production: Kings's Head Th., 15 Aug. 1972.
Published: Five Plays; The Unseen Hand and Other Plays.

Carol and Jim are staying at a camp in the Red Cross cabin. Carol is explaining symptoms she has detected to a disinterested Jim, and tells a story of an imaginary skiing accident that completely dismembered her. A voice offstage calls to her and she leaves to go to town. Jim immediately takes off his trousers and begins picking small bugs out of the skin of his legs and stepping on them. He begins doing push-ups on the floor as the maid comes to the screen door to change the beds. At first Jim won't let her change the beds because he says he is embarrassed by the yellow spots on his sheets. She finally begins to work and Jim asks her if she knows anything about crabs. He continues to interrupt her bed-making and eventually involves her in a swimming lesson on the beds, which takes a nasty turn when the maid imagines that she is drowning. The maid's final speech about drowning and 'coming out of the water in the spring a new creature' leaves Jim frustrated and defeated. The maid leaves, and Carol returns just as Jim gets back into his trousers. Carol explains how she has discovered little bugs all over herself in the bathroom of the grocery store. When Jim turns to face her and the audience there is a stream of blood running down his forehead.

Fourteen Hundred Thousand

One-act play.
First production: Firehouse Th., Minneapolis, 1966
    (dir. Sydney Schubert Walter). Subsequently shown on National
    Educational Television.
Published: Five Plays; The Unseen Hand and Other Plays.

---

*Tom and Donna are building a bookcase for her fourteen
hundred thousand books, assisted or watched by Ed, Mom, and
Pop. They have an argument, slapping at each other with paint
brushes, after which the play changes course. Mom and Pop
recite from the books they are reading, first the story of a great
snowfall (joined by the others), then a prophecy of the 'linear
city'. The others hum 'White Christmas'.*

I was very interested in the idea of the linear city, because it struck me as
being a strong visual conception as opposed to radial cities — the idea
of having a whole country, especially like America, with these lines
cutting across them.

                    Shepard, interview in *Theatre Quarterly*, p. 9

He juxtaposes a naturalistic scene (about the construction of
bookshelves) with a deliberately non-naturalistic, heavily scored section
(in which the virtues of a linear city are extolled in a language whose
constrictive regularities offer an ironic commentary on its subject
matter). But again the subject is, in a sense, subordinated to the pleasure
he takes in controlling not merely language but sound (as the
bookshelves are hammered into place or collapse to the ground) and
light (precisely prescribed lighting changes take place). Indeed, he offers
an oblique defence of his strategy in the form of a brief speech by one of
the characters who sees the pleasure of collecting books precisely in
terms of their size, shape and colour rather than their contents. 'With
various sizes and shapes and groups together. Without concern for what
they're about or what they mean to me and who wrote them when. Just
in terms of size and shape and colour.' The aesthetic is close to that of
the minimalist artist, concerned with colour field, texture and form
rather than narrative content or expressive symbol. To some degree he
also seems to be suggesting that the pleasure lies in the process itself. He

has the abstract expressionist's delight in the action of creation. Thus he has said of his work that it 'is not written in granite. It's like playing a piece of music. It goes out in the air and dissolves forever.'

C.W.E. Bigsby, *A Critical Introduction to Twentieth-Century American Drama, Vol. 3*, p. 225

La Turista

Two-act play.
First production: American Place Th., New York, 4 Mar. 1967
    (dir. Jacques Levy; with Sam Waterston, Joyce Aaron).
First London production: Theatre Upstairs at Royal Court, 18 Mar. 1969
    (dir. Roger Hendricks-Simon).
Published: La Turista (Indianapolis: Bobbs-Merrill, 1968;
    London: Faber, 1969); *Four Two-Act Plays; Seven Plays.*

A young couple, Kent and Salem, lie in a Mexican hotel room suffering from sunburn. Kent, the man, also has 'la turista' (dysentery), and dies at the end of the first act, despite a chicken sacrifice by local witch doctors. The second act has the same elements, but the hotel room is American, the doctor and his son are in Civil War costume, and Kent ends the play by jumping through the upstage wall.

Perhaps the characters are not profitably thought of as characters at all. They are actors, parodists. They slip from style to style; they carry a few props around with them as they change their roles; they 'freeze' when they want to withdraw from the action on stage. The essence of their being is energy, verbal energy. In the restless inventiveness of their parodies and tirades, a storm of feeling and experience blows across the stage. The parts are arias.

Elizabeth Hardwick, review used as Introduction to
La Turista and *Four Two-Act Plays;* also in *American Dreams*, p. 67-71.

See also:
Interviews with Levy and Waterston in Ellen Oumano, *Sam Shepard* (London: Virgin, 1987), p. 49-58; Joyce Aaron, 'Clues in a Memory', in *American Dreams*, p. 171-4.

Melodrama Play

One-act 'melodrama with music'.
First production: La Mama ETC, New York, 18 May 1967
   (dir. Tom O'Horgan).
Revived: by La Mama in 1968, 1971; in rock plays season 'Shep in
   Rep', Horace Mann Th., 1979.
First London production: La Mama European tour, Mercury Th.,
   11 Sept. 1967.
Published: Five Plays; Fool for Love and Other Plays.

*Duke Durgens, a singer-songwriter with one big hit, and his
brother Drake (who really wrote the song) are harassed
violently by Duke's manager and his bodyguard, who try to force
them to produce a follow-up.*

Cowboys No. 2

One-act play.
First production: Mark Taper Forum, Los Angeles, Nov. 1967
   (dir. Edward Parone).
First New York production: Old Reliable, 12 Aug. 1969 (dir. Bill Hart).
First London production: Pindar of Wakefield, July 1972.
*Published: Mad Dog Blues and Other Plays; The Unseen Hand and
   Other Plays.*

*Two young men sit leaning against the upstage wall and talk
about whether it is likely to rain. Then each in turn plays an old-
timer surveying the approaching clouds, watching a rainstorm
rolling in and the mud it creates, fantasizing a still starry prairie
night and an Indian attack. During the attack Stu, who is
playing Clem, is shot with an imaginary arrow, and Chet
(playing Mel) angrily fires on the Indians until they retreat. Chet
throws water from his hat in the wounded Stu's face, and Stu
angrily stops the game, soaks his feet in the stream Chet created
off the edge of the stage and talks about how things have
changed — from orange blossoms to chickens eating their own*

shit and dying and decaying. During this, car horns are heard in the distance. Chet takes over the same position, and has his 'turn' — a long catalogue of breakfast foods and the enjoyment that he gets from them. The car horns increase in volume, and Man One and Man Two have a conversation from the wings across the stage. Chet tries to wake Stu but can't, and Chet moves more and more into his old man, now trying to keep the vultures away from the body of his wounded friend. The car horns are joined by the sounds of the Indian attack, and just before the end of Chet's long, desperate speech the two men enter and sit against the back wall in suits, reading the play from the beginning.

Theatrefacts, No. 3 (1974), p. 6-7

When I directed *Cowboys No. 2* two years ago, one of the problems was to relate the many activities that create the visual image, many of which were unnatural for an actor to perform, to the reality of the play. For it is very important that the games and activities be explored and the level of play established. For example, Stu talks about blood circulation and diabetes while he is doing calisthenics. The connection between the action and what is being talked about is obvious, but often these actions, which are physically difficult, must be performed during a speech and must still have spontaneity. There are often strenuous physical demands made on the actors in Sam's plays, usually during important speeches that need their concentration — when the two men play 'old-timers' celebrating the long-awaited rain by dancing and playing in the mud; or when, having finally reached the Red Valley, they are attacked by Indians.

Here the actor must create in his imagination and the imagination of the audience those film sequences that inspire children to play cowboys and indians. This demands that the actor throw himself into the role with childlike abandon and great intensity. But in the same way that a child can stop in the middle of a game and be himself, so an actor playing a man playing an 'old-timer' being attacked by Indians must be able to stop at any time and be the man or the actor. For *Cowboys No. 2* is about two men who are talking to one another, remembering not only their own pasts, but also a collective past. Whether any of it is true doesn't matter; what matters is that it is a part of our experience and Shepard has shaped it into a series of images that flash film-like across the stage.

Kenneth Chubb, 'Fruitful Difficulties of Directing Shepard',
Theatre Quarterly, IV, No. 15 (1974), p. 19

Forensic and the Navigators

One-act play.
First production: Theatre Genesis, New York, 29 Dec. 1967
    (dir. Ralph Cook; with Lee Kissman, O-Lan Shepard).
Revived: Off-Broadway in double bill with *The Unseen Hand*, Astor
    Place Th., 1 Apr. 1970.
Published: The Unseen Hand and Other Plays.

---

*A somewhat confused struggle between two revolutionaries and
the Exterminators, who are agents for an unnamed power
holding people in a nearby prison camp. Neither side is very
resolute in this struggle, as they are easily distracted by the
charms of a very young girl, Oolan. As they drift in their
confusion, they are destroyed by a cloud of coloured gas which
covers the stage and billows out over the audience. The foes
remain in an interminable state of stasis.*

Ellen Oumano, *Sam Shepard*
(London: Virgin, 1987), p. 68

The Holy Ghostly

One-act play.
First production: La Mama European tour, 1969
    (dir. Tom O'Horgan).
First American production: New Troupe at McCarter Th.,
    Princeton, New Jersey, Jan. 1970 (dir. Tom O'Horgan).
First London production: King's Head Th., July 1973.
Published: The Unseen Hand and Other Plays.

---

*Ice has come from New York to camp out with his father Pop
and try to catch the ghostly Chindi. The Chindi appears, and so
does a witch, who leaves Pop's corpse with them. In one of their
endless arguments, Ice shoots Pop. In dying, he throws his
corpse into the campfire, and then joins it, dancing. 'The whole
theatre is consumed in flames' as he chants 'Burn! Burn!'.*

The Unseen Hand

One-act play.

First production: La Mama ETC, New York, 26 Dec. 1969
  (dir. Jeff Bleckner; with Lee Kissman, Beeson Carroll).
Revived: with *Forensic and the Navigators*, details as above;
  Perry St. Th., 1977; La Mama, 1982.
First London production: Theatre Upstairs, Royal Court, 12 Mar. 1973
  (dir. Jim Sharman).
Published: Action and The Unseen Hand (includes introduction on
  'Azusa' by Shepard); *The Unseen Hand and Other Plays.*

Blue Morphan, a relic of the Old West, sprawls in a derelict car near a highway in Azusa, California. Willie the Space Freak appears, and reveals that he has come to persuade the Morphan brothers, bandits in the last century, to liberate the planet Nogo. The other brothers arrive but so does the Kid, a high school cheerleader, who eventually tries to take these 'subversives' prisoner. He falls victim to the hand which causes Willie's seizures; declaring himself free, Willie returns to Nogo.

Everybody's caught up in a fractured world that they can't even see. What's happening is unfathomable but they have a suspicion. Something unseen is working on them, using them. They have no power and all the time they believe they're controlling the situation.

Shepard

Mr Shepard is perhaps the first person to write good disposable plays. He may well go down in history as the man who was to drama what Kleenex was to the handkerchief. And just like Kleenex, he may well overcome. ... Mr. Shepard takes an apocalyptic view of our civilization, and yet, disconcertingly, instead of moralizing at us, he tells us anecdotal jokes, shaggy-dog stories ...

Clive Barnes, *New York Times*, 2 Apr. 1970, p. 43

He continues to confront American popular culture with a kind of manic exuberance — not exalting its every wart and pimple, like Andy Warhol, but nevertheless considerable turned on, like many of his generation,

even by its more brutalized expressions. In a degenerate time, this may
be a strategy for survival, and it certainly sparks the energy of *The
Unseen Hand*; but I miss that quality of aloofness that would make this
play not only a creative act, but an act of moral resistance as well.

Robert Brustein, *The Observer*, 18 Mar. 1973

See also:
Jim Sharman, 'It'll Get You In the End', *Plays and Players*, May 1973,
p. xiii-xv.
David Savran, 'Sam Shepard's Conceptual Prison: *Action* and
The Unseen Hand', *Theatre Journal*, XXXVI, No. 1 (Mar. 1984),
p. 57-74.
Interview with Albert Poland (producer) in Ellen Oumano,
Sam Shepard (London: Virgin, 1987), p. 79-85.

Operation Sidewinder

Two-act play with music.
First production: Vivian Beaumont Th., Lincoln Center, New York,
12 Mar. 1970 (dir. Michael A. Schultz). The play was due to be
staged at Yale in early 1969, but Shepard withdrew rights after
protests over the portrayal of black revolutionaries.
Published: Operation Sidewinder (Indianapolis: Bobbs-Merrill, 1970);
Four Two-Act Plays; *The Unseen Hand and Others Plays*. Earlier
version in *Esquire*, May 1969.

*An advanced US Air Force computer, shaped like a sidewinder
snake, escapes into the desert where it becomes the heart of a
battle between the power-crazed military and a group of black
revolutionaries intent on using drugs to take over the country.
When an Indian tribe gains possession of the computer, however,
it integrates it into a spiritual rule which is derived partly from
its own painful history and partly from beings from outer space
who, at the moment of apocalypse, rescue from the detritus of
modern civilization only those who retain a vestige of spiritual
integrity. The satirical edge, reminiscent of Terry Southern,
which mocks American society with a free-ranging vigour, is
balanced by a sentimental vision which wishes to locate human*

values in some irrecoverable past, or in the lyrical insights of the young and the music with which they counter the mechanical sounds of a civilization in decline.

Theatrefacts, No. 3 (1974), p. 8

Shepard's theatrical world is like a surrealist painting; a dream landscape where the sights and sounds are at once logical and familiar, outrageous and threatening: a six-foot sidewinder which is really an escaped military computer; black, white and Indian renegades plotting to capture Air Force planes by putting dope in a military reservoir; a Hopi snake dance whose ritual transforms the sidewinder computer from military equipment to religious icon. There is a discomforting cerebral weirdness beneath each character's surface clarity: a mystery and obsession which are the wounds of the society. ... With *Operation Sidewinder* Shepard leads us through a grotesque spectacle of our psychic death, and the possibility of rebirth'.

John Lahr, *Village Voice*, 19 Mar. 1970, p. 43-4

How does the play go wrong? Its absurdist technique is seldom funny enough and, all too often, lapses into earnest preachment. I surmise that absurdist playwriting ... is suitable only for swift, dazzling, one-act phantasmagoria, and refuses to stretch to full-length plays.

John Simon, 'More Ordinance than Ordonnance',
New York, 30 Mar. 1970, p. 56

Operation Sidewinder dramatizes the yearning for a new history and the search for new symbols to inhabit the world. Like the Young Man, Shepard is fascinated by Indian culture. The apocalyptic vision prophesied by the Spider Lady is acted out on the stage — a fantasy enactment of our cosmic longings and fears, as in a science-fiction thriller. This theatrical tactic reflects Shepard's own desire to have symbols transformed from death-giving to life-giving.

John Lahr, 'Spectacle of Disintegration', in *American Dreams*, p. 55

See also:

Clive Barnes, 'Stage: Lizard vs. Snake', *New York Times*, 13 Mar. 1970, p. 33.

Walter Kerr, ' "I Am! I Am!" He Cries — But Am He?', *New York Times*, 22 Mar. 1970.

Robert Brustein, *Making Scenes* (New York: Random House, 1981), p. 73-79.

Shaved Splits

One-act play.
First production: La Mama ETC, New York, July 1970 (dir. Bill Hart).
Published: The Unseen Hand and Other Plays (1971).

This one begins with [Cherry] stretched out on an enormous pink bed in a brilliantly pink bedroom, reading a little paperback pornography. It ends with a hippie revolutionary, who has been battling the police single-handedly for some time from Cherry's boudoir, delivering a fantasy monologue about the West and the simpler virtues of other days. In between there's a lot of violence, but it's neutral violence, it neither really improves nor worsens things.

Arthur Sainer, *Village Voice*, 6 Aug. 1970

Mad Dog Blues

'Two-act adventure show' with music.
First production: Theatre Genesis at St Mark's Church-in-the Bowery, New York, 4 Mar. 1971 (dir. Robert Glaudini).
Revived: in 'Shep in Rep', Horace Mann Th., 1979.
Published: Mad Dog Blues and Other Plays; The Unseen Hand and Other Plays.

Rock star Kosmo, a country boy who aches for the West, and his sidekick Yahoodi, a city slicker strung out on dope, conjure up images of Marlene Dietrich and Mae West (though a Mae West who sings like Janis Joplin) and set off on an adventure. Yahoodi and Marlene join Captain Kidd in his search for buried treasure, and Kosmo and Mae secretly follow them along with an old-timer they've picked up named Waco Texas. After Mae leaves him for Paul Bunyan, Yahoodi shoots himself and Captain Kidd, so Kosmo and Mae steal the treasure, which turns out to be a bunch of bottle caps.

Don Shewey, *Sam Shepard* (New York: Dell, 1985), p. 78

See also:
Mel Gussow, *New York Times*, 9 Mar. 1971, p. 25.
George Stambolian, 'Shepard's *Mad Dog Blues*: a Trip Through Popular
    Culture', *Journal of Popular Culture*, VII, No. 4 (Spring 1974);
    reprinted in *American Dreams*, p. 79-89.

Cowboy Mouth

One-act play with music. Written with Patti Smith.
First production: Traverse Th., Edinburgh, 12 Apr. 1971
    (dir. Gordon Stewart).
First American production: American Place Th., 29 Apr. 1971
    (dir. Robert Glaudini, with Sam Shepard, Patti Smith).
First London production: King's Head Th., July 1972.
Revived: 'Shep in Rep', 1979; Wonderhorse Th., 1981.
*Published: Mad Dog Blues and Other Plays; Fool for Love and
    Other Plays.*

*Cavale, a woman with a taste for French poetry, wants to turn
Slim into a rock and roll star. They play fantasy games, argue,
and order food, delivered by a Lobster Man in lobster costume.
During his second visit his shell cracks open, revealing him to
be the 'rock-and-roll saviour'. He puts a pistol to his head, but it
merely clicks when he pulls the trigger.*

Back Bog Beast Bait

One-act play with music.
First production: American Place Th., New York, 29 Apr. 1971
    (dir. Tony Barsha, with Beeson Carroll, O-Lan Shepard).
Revived: La Mama, 1984 (dir. George Ferencz; with jazz score by
    Max Roach).
Published: The Unseen Hand and Other Plays.

*Two cowboys, Slim and Shadow, are hired by a woman to fight a
monster ravaging the Louisiana countryside. The other
characters are a Preacher, and the witch-girl Gris Gris, who*

both contribute to the apocalyptic atmosphere. When the 'pig-beast' finally appears, all five are transformed into appropriate animals.

See also:
Mel Gussow, 'Shepard's Prophetic "Beast" Retains its Bite',
   New York Times, 16 Dec. 1984, Sect. 2, p. 3, 34.

The Tooth of Crime

Two-act play with music.
First production: Open Space Th., London, 17 July 1972
   (dir. Charles Marowitz and Walter Donohue; music composed by
   Shepard).
First American production: McCarter Th., Princeton University,
   11 Nov. 1972.
Revived: Performance Group at Performing Garage, New York,
   7 Mar. 1973 (dir. Richard Schechner; a film of this 'environmental'
   production was made for the Whitney Museum); Royal Court,
   London, 5 June 1974 (dir. Jim Sharman); 'Shep in Rep', 1979, and
   La Mama, New York, 1983 (both dir. George Ferencz); Black Theatre
   Co-operative at Croydon Warehouse, London, 15 Sept. 1983;
   Bridge Lane Th., London, 5 June 1987.
Published: Four Two-Act Plays; Seven Plays.

Hoss in black leather rocker gear sings the first song in a room where the only piece of furniture is a large black chair with silver studs. Becky brings him an assortment of revolvers, pistols and rifles, and they talk of a planned move. Hoss consults the Star-Man, who warns Hoss that the moon chart is unfavourable. The language they use is a combination of criminal, rock, motor-car-racing, astrological and old-west jargons and Hoss's planned move seems to combine the worlds of these jargons. Galactic Jack, the disc-jockey, helps to encourage Hoss to advance, but Hoss is uneasy about many things. Vegas has been 'rolled' and it was on Hoss's tickets, and it turns out that one of the 'Gypsies' has 'marked' Hoss. Cheyenne, Hoss's driver, can offer no advice to him in dealing with the Gypsy, and Hoss takes a shot from the Doc to cool himself down. Hoss rehearses a knife fight and Becky sings to him to ease the tension. The first act ends with the announcement that the Gypsy has arrived. Crow, the Gypsy, is of a new generation, a Keith Richard type with an eye patch, chewing gum and swirling a short silver chain. Hoss offers Crow some wine, and while he is getting it Crow tries to copy his walk. The duel is to be musical, and there is to be a prior sussing-out period, in which a slip in jargon or in assurance scores. By now Crow has sussed Hoss's walk exactly, and this gives him an advantage. A National Basketball Association referee is called in, and round by round they alternate songs with Crow finally declared the winner. Hoss offers Crow all his territory if he will teach Hoss the new style, but Hoss finds it difficult. Becky has a dream-like scene in which she is 'parking' with a boy, probably a younger Hoss, who is trying to seduce her. Hoss realizes the newer style isn't him and shoots himself. Crow takes over, keeping Becky but dismissing Cheyenne, who leaves him the keys to the Masarati. Crow sings the final song.

Theatrefacts, No. 3 (1974), p. 10

Most rock plays are just Broadway versions of rock 'n' roll. A real rock play would have to be at least as good as The Who. Meaning at least as overtly violent.

Shepard

It's a failure as a play. Overall it doesn't have a totality or a cohesiveness. I let it drift too much. And there is a confusion of styles; trying to be a musical, and an avant-garde piece, and a Brecht piece, all at the same time.

Shepard

It's an interesting thing that happened with that play, because I wrote it in London — it's been called an American play, right, but it was written in the middle of Shepherd's Bush, and for about a month before that I was struggling to write this other play called *The Tooth of Crime*, which was a three-act epic number in a jail ... and at the end it was a complete piece of shit, so I put it in the sink and burnt it, and then an hour later I started to write this one that's been performed. ...It started with language — it started with hearing a certain sound which is coming from the voice of this character, Hoss, and also this sort of black figure appearing on stage with this throne, and the whole kind of world that he was involved in, came from this voice — I don't mean it was any weird psychological voice in the air thing, but that it was a very real kind of sound that I heard, and I started to write the play from there. It just accumulated force as I wrote it.

Shepard, interview in *Theatre Quarterly*, p. 11

The battle of song between Hoss and Crow is fairly diverting, and the referee has the sense to stop the fight before boredom supervenes ... but the defeat of one pop style by another — is that all there is? And if the moral is that those who live by style shall perish by it, it rebounds onto the play itself. ... In this play Mr. Shepard is as much a prisoner of his language as ever Christopher Fry was.

Robert Cushman, *Plays and Players*, Sept. 1972, p. 45

Americans have an insatiable appetite for victory. ... In this ruthlessly competitive society, it is not surprising that a psychopathic style — the cool, guiltless, violent pursuit of immediate needs — should be the stuff of legend. Street hustlers turned revolutionary prophets; mafioso rubouts; cowboys riding roughshod over untamed land — these are the neurotic tales of America. The aggressive, anti-social style of the psychopath is a survival kit and a sickness. This is the pathology Sam Shepard explores in his exciting verbal tour de force *Tooth of Crime*, a tale of vindictive triumph which mixes the metaphors of car-racing, pop music, and street-fighting.

John Lahr, *Village Voice*, 8 Mar. 1973, p. 55

The play is about the use of style as a weapon. ... It is an intensely American play in the sense that it reflects a disposable, quick-turnover culture. ... It is also American in that it is thoroughly inside the system. Shepard constructs an ambitious stage metaphor, drawing together several strands of American life, to produce an image of insensate brutality. But, having done so, he conveys no judgement or attitude towards it. It is a camp piece, intended as much to raise giggles as to repel.

Irving Wardle, *The Times*, 18 July 1972, p. 11

Mr. Shepard has gathered his forces and produced a splendidly provocative play. ... In *The Tooth of Crime* he has found a mythic subject perfect for his particular dramatic method. ... The implications of the play, its depths and layers, are almost tantalizing. ... The language, hip, original, unexpected and rhythmic, flows in and out of the music.

Clive Barnes, *New York Times*, 12 Dec. 1972, p. 77

Tooth is basically a very simple play. It's even a universal one. The plot might come from Shakespeare: an ageing king goes against the advice of his retinue of advisers and retainers, engages in a duel with a usurper and loses, killing himself to preserve his honour.

Victoria Radin, *The Observer*, 9 June 1974, p. 31

See also:

Richard Schechner, 'The Writer and the Performance Group — Rehearsing *The Tooth of Crime*', *Performance,* No. 5 (Mar.-Apr. 1973); reprinted in *American Dreams*, p. 162-8.

Richard Schechner, 'Drama, Script, Theatre and Performance', *Drama Review*, XVII, No. 3 (Sept. 1973), p. 5-36.

Michael Bloom, 'The Transformation of Realism in Sam Shepard's *Tooth of Crime*', *Exchange*, III, No. 3 (Fall 1977), p. 19-26.

Robert Coe, 'Image Shots Are Blown: the Rock Plays', in *American Dreams*, p. 57-66.

Gautam Dasgupta, 'An Interview with Spalding Gray' (about playing Hoss in Schechner's production), in *American Dreams*, p. 175-83.

Blue Bitch

One-act play.
First American production: Theatre Genesis, 1973
    (dir. Murray Mednick).
Television production: 'Open House', BBC Television, Spring 1973.
Unpublished.

Dixie and Cody, expatriate Americans living in London, are discussing whether or not to sell their greyhound, Breeze (which they've advertised in Sporting Life*), when the phone rings — someone in Scotland wants to buy the bitch and have her sent* *straightaway by train. The Scotsman keeps ringing back, offering more money, but the couple can't make up their minds. Selling the dog is somehow tied up with going to Wyoming. Seemingly as a last resort, they corner the milkman to ask his opinion. Before giving it, however, the milkman seems to 'turn' into a dog and carries on a 'woof' and 'growl' conversation with the Scotsman, after which, returned to normal, he advises them to sell. The play ends with a singing telegram from Wyoming.*

Geography of a Horse Dreamer

'A Mystery in Two Acts'.
First production: Theatre Upstairs, Royal Court, London, 21 Feb. 1974
    (dir. Shepard; with Bob Hoskins, Stephen Rea).
First New York production: Manhattan Th. Club, 4 Dec. 1975
    (dir. Jacques Levy).
Revived: Ensemble Studio Th., 1981; La Mama, 1985.
Published: Four Two-Act Plays; Fool for Love and Other Plays.

Cody, a Wyoming cowboy who has the gift of dreaming the winners of horse races, has been kidnapped by gamblers. But he's losing his gift, he can't dream winners any more, and in desperation the gamblers switch to dog racing. Cody's gift immediately returns, but he soon goes mad, and just as the gamblers are about to remove the 'dream bone' from his neck, his two country brothers burst into the room, murder the gamblers, and take him back to Wyoming.

Ross Wetzsteon, *Village Voice*, 5 Jan. 1976, reprinted as
'Looking a Gift Horse Dreamer in the Mouth',
in *American Dreams*, p. 133-5

I was using language from Raymond Chandler, from Dashiell Hammett — from the 'thirties, which to me is a very beautiful kind of language.

Shepard

Horse Dreamer was too much in the fable genre and created a distance between the audience. I want people to leave my plays with a sense of questioning, a sense of mystery, but not mystification.

Shepard

The characters' names are by no means fortuitous. Cody is clearly named for Buffalo Bill Cody and the Doc for Doc Holliday, but beneath the deliberate mythic resonances is a familiar homily about alienation and lost powers. Fingers is a kind of Godot/God. At first he is simply an absent force: 'We're like his mirror. We never see him but we're always in touch.' The petty gangsters simply follow instructions, live out determined lives, trapped in their own myths: 'it's like a snake bitin' its own tail.' ... The magic which exists within the individual is deflected, destroyed. *Geography of a Horse Dreamer*, like *The Tooth of Crime*, is a threnody, a lament for a lost dream. Cody's dream of the Midwest is forced to defer to a simple mechanism for making money. For Shepard, much the same process has typified America, and since he now locates his play in England — a country in which gambling is described as a national pastime ('The government has hooks directly into the bookmakers. There's protection on every level except for the bums. The police are paid off by high syndicates. For the rich it's a sport. For the poor it's a disease.') — this is offered as simply a modern condition. Though rescued by his brothers, Cody, pure at heart but destroyed in spirit, cannot recapture the world he has lost.

C.W.E. Bigsby, *A Critical Introduction to Twentieth-Century American Drama, Vol. 3*, p. 237

Little Ocean

One-act play.
First production: Hampstead Th. Club, London, 25 Mar. 1974
   (dir. Stephen Rea, with O-Lan Shepard).
Unpublished.

An almost revue-style play with music, very gentle and unlike most of Shepard's work. Three girls — one who has had a child, one who is very pregnant, and one who never has been — look at pregnancy from an ironically humorous, often frustrated modern woman's point of view. The actresses create settings as and when they need them — a room, a park — and act out fantasies and frustrations that have to do with pregnancy: sudden vacillations of emotion, an angry turn with a baby carriage and a squalling infant, a child making idiots of its parents, nasty kids in a park threatening the three women with stones. The central image of the little ocean refers to the child's vast playground within the womb.

Theatrefacts, No. 3 (1974), p. 11

Action

One-act play.
First production: American Place Th., 15 Apr. 1975, in a double bill with *Killer's Head* (dir. Nancy Meckler).
Revived: Magic Th., San Francisco, Spring 1975 (dir. Shepard).
Published: Action and The Unseen Hand; Fool for Love and Other Plays.

Two girls and two men in jeans with shaven heads seated round a wooden table wait for and finally consume a real roasted turkey. From time to time some small but shattering event — as when the bulkier man, known as Jeep, is moved by a sudden urge to smash his chair to pieces — punctuates a meal which proceeds with the deliberation, at once motiveless and purposeful, of a chimpanzees' tea party.

Hilary Spurling, *The Observer*, 22 Sept. 1974, p. 26

Groping for significance, Shepard has coughed up a rehash of recent reading, a combination of Beckett's angst with Peter Handke's scenic still-life. ... Action, Shepard is saying, is a mechanism through which man fills the void. Sadly, in this play, the action merely adds to the void. ... *Action* has no mystery, only obfuscation, no characters, only fragments of speech. It is a dead end, not only for its gifted playwright but for the audience.

John Lahr, *Village Voice*, 31 Oct. 1974, p. 90

See also:
Benedict Nightingale, *New Statesman*, 27 Sept. 1974, p. 440.

John Simon, *New York,* 5 May 1975, p. 94.
David Savran, 'Sam Shepard's Conceptual Prison: *Action* and *The Unseen Hand*', *Theatre Journal,* XXXVI, No. 1 (Mar. 1984), p. 57-74.

Killer's Head

A monologue.
First production: American Place Th., New York, 15 Apr. 1975, in a double bill with *Action* (dir. Nancy Meckler, with Richard Gere).
Published: The Unseen Hand and Other Plays.

Killer's Head, *an innocent boyish thing about the nurturing of a racehorse, made horrifying by the fact that it represents the last thoughts of a young man about to be electrocuted.*

Michael Feingold, *Village Voice,* 21 Apr. 1975

Angel City

Two-act play with music.
First production: Magic Th., San Francisco, 2 July 1976 (dir. Shepard; with music by Bob Feldman).
First New York production: Second Company of the Williamstown Th. Festival, Playwrights Horizons, 21 Oct. 1977.
First London production: New End Th., 23 Sept. 1983 (dir. Adrian Jackson).
Revived: Theatre Genesis, 1978; Wonderhorse Th., 1982; La Mama, 1984.
Published: Angel City and Other Plays; Fool for Love and Other Plays.

Angel City refers to Hollywood and greater Los Angeles. It shows up Shepard's fascination with movie making and celluloid tycoons, though he also sees the city and its business as heading for apocalypse. So Rabbit Brown a young magician and fixer ... is summoned to a Hollywood studio to work a 'slight miracle' on a disaster movie. ... As if in debt to Ionesco's Rhinoceros — *though not with the same sharp sense of purpose — everyone is being turned into snakes and lizards, with one of the executives, Wheeler, already nastily en route to transformation. Disaster in the script runs in parallel with disaster outside and eventually movie and life seem destined to become one, while on the sidelines a tympanist ... acts as a crazy chorus of doom with his instrument.*

Nicholas de Jongh, *The Guardian*, 24 Sept. 1983

[In Hollywood] you're riding on the surface of the ocean and underneath it are all kinds of monsters which everybody either ignores or conceals. ... Hollywood is dead set against recognizing the fact that if a writer writes something, he has to do it on his own.

Shepard

There is a witty inventiveness to Shepard's characters — Rabbit Brown with his Indian bones and totems, the star-struck secretary Miss Spoons wishing herself the other side of the silver screen, the movie producer literally festering with poisonous ideas, and Tympani employed solely to tap his drums until he comes up with an undiscovered rhythm which will hypnotize audiences.

The trouble is that the Hollywood dream machine is anyway such a parody of itself that Sam Shepard is provoked to desperate flights of fancy to mythologize it. In consequence, *Angel City* loses touch with the dream-logic which drives his better plays and ends up somewhere between farce and satire, with characters made to jump through too many hoops to hold our interest.

Christopher Hudson, *Evening Standard*, 24 Sept. 1983

See also:
Carol Rosen, 'Sam Shepard's *Angel City*: a Movie for the Stage', *Modern Drama*, XXII, No. 1 (Mar. 1979), p. 39-46.

Suicide in B^b

'A Mysterious Overture' in one act with music.
First production: Yale Repertory Th., New Haven, 15 Oct. 1976
    (dir. Walt Jones; with music by Lawrence Wolf).
First New York production: Impossible Ragtime Th., Mar. 1979
    (dir. Ted Story; with music by Mitchell Weiss).

First London production: Open Space Th., Oct. 1977
   (dir. Kenneth Chubb).
Revived: La Mama, 1984, in 'Shepard Sets' with *Angel City* and
   Back Bog Beast Bait (dir. George Ferencz; with jazz score by
   Max Roach).
*Published: Buried Child and Seduced and Suicide in B^b; Fool for Love
   and Other Plays.*

---

*The play takes the form of an improvisation, within the genre of
pulp fiction. Two detectives, with mysterious links to government
agencies, are trying to solve a mystery regarding Niles, a
celebrated jazz composer, whose corpse has been found in his
room. Was his death the result of murder or suicide? ... When
these conventional-minded working stiffs are joined by a
suicidal female bass player and a skinny spaced-out saxophonist
who blows soundless music ... the whole business begins to get
beyond them ... Niles appears, invisible to all except a nervous
young groupie who accompanies him ... he must annihilate a
series of identities that prevent him achieving authenticity. By
the end of the play, Niles has walked through the walls of his
room to accept responsibility for his own death.*
Robert Brustein, Critical Moments
(New York: Random House, 1980), p. 118-19

The idea of dying and being reborn is really an interesting one, you
know. It's always there at the back of my head.
Shepard

See also:
Jon Pareles, on 'Shepard Sets' season, *New York Times*, 18 Nov. 1984,
   Sec. 2, p. 4, 20.

The Sad Lament of Pecos Bill on the Eve of Killing His Wife

All-sung music drama in one act.
First production: Bay Area Playwrights Festival, San Francisco,

22 Oct. 1976 (dir. Robert Woodruff; with music by Shepard and Catherine Stone).

First New York production: La Mama ETC, in a double bill with *Superstitions*, Sept. 1983 (dir. Julie Hebert).

Published: Fool for Love and The Sad Lament.

An operetta about the first cowboy and his wife, Slue-foot Sue, whom he killed by allowing her to ride his horse, which threw her fifty feet, so she 'cracked the sky and had to duck the moon'. At the opening, Pecos Bill enters dragging behind him the body of Slue-foot Sue, lying on a mattress on the back of some gigantic insect or animal. She jumps down and joins him in his lament for the passing of his own legend and of the Old West that nurtured it, filling in his descriptions of his exploits.

Edith Oliver, *New Yorker*, 26 Sept. 1983, p. 126

See also:

Benedict Nightingale, 'Even Minimal Shepard Is Food For Thought', *New York Times*, 25 Sept. 1983, Sec. 2, p. 5, 26.

Inacoma

Play with music.
First production: Magic Th., San Francisco, 18 Mar. 1977 (dir. Shepard).
Unpublished.

Collaborative and partly improvised play about a woman in a coma and those around her, loosely based on the Karen Ann Quinlan case. Shepard determined overall structure, and provided song lyrics and speeches.

See also:

William Kleb, 'Sam Shepard's *Inacoma* at the Magic Theatre', *Theater,* IX, No. 1 (Fall 1977).

Roger Downey, 'Inside the Words' (interview with Shepard), *Time Out*, 22-28 Apr. 1977, p. 11.

Curse of the Starving Class

Three-act play.
First production: Royal Court, London, 21 Apr. 1977
   (dir. Nancy Meckler).
First American production: New York Shakespeare Festival, Public Th.,
   2 Mar. 1978 (dir. Robert Woodruff).
Revived: Image Th., 1983; Promenade Th., 1985.
Published: Angel City and Other Plays; Seven Plays.

---

*The family — the son and daughter, the mother and a father who
appears partway through — live in a kind of hellish chaos. Their
household is a ramshackle, collapsing affair somewhere in the
West. ... The household is disintegrating. The mother tries to run
off to Europe or Mexico, but ends up asleep on the table. The
daughter wants to run off to become a car mechanic. ... The son
has an inchoate obsession with keeping the family together, and
the father rallies at one point, bathes, sobers up, does the laun-
dry and tries to head off the growing chaos. Ultimately a gang
of murderous creditors takes over, blows up the family car with
the daughter inside it, and seems determined to kill the father ...*
Richard Eder, *New York Times*, 3 Mar. 1978, Sec. C, p. 3

See also:
John Lahr, *Plays and Players*, June 1977, p. 24-5.
Roger Downey, 'Inside the Words' (interview with Shepard), *Time Out*,
   22-28 Apr. 1977, p. 11.
Stanley Kauffmann, 'What Price Freedom?', *New Republic*,
   8 Apr. 1978, reprinted in *American Dreams*, p. 104-07.

Seduced

Two-act play.
First production: Trinity Sq. Repertory Co., Providence R.I., Apr. 1978.
First New York production: American Place Th., 1 Feb. 1979
   (dir. Jack Gelber, with Rip Torn).
First London production: Th. Upstairs, 16 May 1980 (dir. Les Waters).
*Published: Buried Child and Seduced and Suicide in B^b; Fool for Love
   and Other Plays.*

The last hours of an enfeebled and eccentric wealthy recluse,
obviously suggested by the late Howard Hughes, is the subject
of Seduced. ... *The action occurs in his sealed hotel suite in an*
unnamed Caribbean country, to which he summons two former
mistresses (or possibly ex-wives) in an attempt to kindle his
failing appetite for life. ... An obsequious bodyguard humours
the eccentric codger until the play's climax, when he attempts to
force his charge to deed over his vast financial holdings. The
aide's final shooting of the hero has no effect, since the weirdo
recluse suddenly turns ethereal.

Richard Hummler, *Variety*, 7 Feb. 1979, p. 112

Buried Child

Three-act play, winner of Pulitzer Prize for Drama, 1979.
First production: Magic Th., San Francisco, 27 June 1978
   (dir. Robert Woodruff).
First New York production: Theater for the New City, 19 Oct. 1978
   (dir. Robert Woodruff; later transferred to Th. de Lys).
First London production: Hampstead Th. Club, 19 June 1980
   (dir. Nancy Meckler).
Revived: Yale, 1979; Circle Rep., 1979.
Published: Buried Child and Seduced and Suicide in B^b; Seven Plays.

A midwestern farm gone to seed. ... Grandfather Dodge is a
sedentary cougher solaced only by television and whisky.
Grandmother Halie in Whistlerian black flirts with a clergyman
to promote a statue for her dead son. More or less alive are her
sons Tilden, an ex-football star and present half-wit, and
Bradley, a sadistic cripple before whom the others cower. Home
to the family bosom come grandson musician Vince and his
California girlfriend. Appalled though he is by this return to his
roots, Vince decides to remain and face his dubious heritage.
His father Tilden, having dug up carrots and corn from the
backyard, ends the play carrying the decayed corpse of a buried
child. Realistically, Dodge has murdered his wife's probably
incestuous infant, but symbolically youth is buried by the

American family — incestuous, idiotic, sadistic, and moribund.
Ruby Cohn, *New American Dramatists 1960-1980*
(London: Macmillan, 1982), p. 184-5

It's sort of a typical Pulitzer Prize-winning play. It wasn't written for that purpose; it was kind of a test. I wanted to write a play about a family.
Shepard

What doesn't have to do with family? There isn't anything. Even a love story has to do with family. Crime has to do with family. We all come out of each other — everyone is born out of a mother and father. It's an endless cycle.

Shepard

This is the best Shepard play I have seen in some time, which means that it is powerful, obsessive stuff, intensely theatrical, not always disciplined but always wildly poetic, full of stage images and utterances replete with insidious suggestiveness even if they don't yield unequivocal meanings. ... Here as in other Shepard works, the effect is rather as if Pieter Breughel and Hieronymous Bosch had set about improving a Grant Wood canvas, until rustic creepiness grew into manic vitality and visionary madness. The one sane outsider who wanders into the familial, do-it-yourself inferno in which the action is laid is helplessly torn between acute, incredulous fascination and the fearful need to run for the sake of her sanity, indeed life.
John Simon, *New York*, 27 Nov. 1978, p. 118

The buried child of the title, though actual, reminds us of the imaginary child in *Who's Afraid of Virginia Woolf?* It is a dark secret, whose existence is never to be acknowledged in public. Although the play deals with a homecoming — one of several points in common with Harold Pinter — it is equally connected to Edward Albee. This is an American nightmare in which an ingrown family bastions itself against invading reality. Mr. Shepard is a playwright of the American frontier, but his plays generally take place in confined, even claustrophobic, rooms.
Mel Gussow, *New York Times*, 2 Jan. 1979, p. C7

An odd play for Shepard, in the sense that his plays have always been identifiable by their striking originality. This one has the most echoes of

39

plays of other writers: Ibsen's *Ghosts*, Pinter's *Homecoming*, and Albee's *The American Dream* come immediately to mind. *Buried Child* is a three-act realistic drama for a post-absurdist age. It is a kind of realism textured with the surreal as only Shepard can do it.

Bonnie Marranca, 'Sam Shepard',
in Bonnie Marranca, Gautam Dasgupta,
American Playwrights: a Critical Survey, p. 108

See also:

Walter Kerr, 'Sam Shepard — What's the Message?', *New York Times*, 10 Dec. 1978, Sec. D, p. 3.

Robert Coe, 'Interview with Robert Woodruff', in *American Dreams*, p. 153-7.

Tongues

'A piece for voice and percussion' by Shepard and Joseph Chaikin.
First production: Magic Th., San Francisco, Summer 1978
    (Chaikin as Speaker, Shepard as percussionist and director).
First New York production: in a double bill with *Savage/Love*,
    Public Th., Nov. 1979; performed by Chaikin, dir. Robert Woodruff).
Published: Seven Plays.

On his deathbed, a man hears voices and sees visions from his past and from his future — from birth to death. He has conversations with himself, dialogue buzzing like mosquitoes around his ears.

Mel Gussow, 'Theater: a Shepard-Chaikin Joint Effort',
New York Times, 16 Nov. 1979, Sec. C, p. 6

Savage/Love

Piece for solo performance with music, by Shepard and Joseph Chaikin, with music by Harry Mann and Skip La Plante.
First New York production: in a double bill with *Tongues*, Public Th., as above (dir. Shepard).
*First London production:*Donmar Warehouse, 30 Apr. 1984
    (dir. Christopher Payton).
Published: Seven Plays.

Television production: PBS Television, 1985 (dir. Shirely Clarke).

Joseph Chaikin twists and turns as if he is fighting to go to sleep or wrestling with his dreams. Soon he is 'tangled deep in love ... in sleep' and he is telling himself a post-bedtime story. This is a love story and it moves from tentative first meeting through courtship, conflict, and the ennui of extended familiarity. We hear about the character's insecurity, his need for affection, and the changes that he goes through in the active pursuit of a continuing relationship. ... The story rambles like a dream. It stops and starts: the actor suddenly becomes frozen and inarticulate. Then once again the flow begins.

Mel Gussow, 'Theater', as above

Alas for expectation. *Savage/Love*, subtitled 'Common poems of real and imagined moments in the spell of love,' consists of acted recitations of indifferent free verse by a man and woman on a stage furnished with two actors' make-up tables and a large double bed.

They prowl around in the half-dark, verbalizing solemnly about sex and love and the way each trammels the other, or else just chatting. She cannot decide whether to call him darling, sugar or treasure. He broods throatily on the moment he first saw her.

Or they dance playfully, ask coy questions, or pretend one is injured — 'we're not saying which.' They fantasize about killing one another and finally realize (I think) that their love has been murdered — but how or by whom we do not know.

Perhaps if Mr. Chaikin had been around, he would have seen to it that Garry Cooper gave us more than a handsome face, and Caroline Quentin more than a self-satisfied languor and would have made clear what the work was trying to say.

John Barber, *Daily Telegraph*, 1 May 1984

Perceptions ... don't automatically make poems; nor do poems, albeit artfully linked, make much of an evening in the theatre. Only a couple of times did I feel the occasion rose above a modish stylishness. Once was when Mr. Cooper in 'Watching the Sleeping Lover', hovered over Ms. Quentin on a heart-shaped bed with a mixture of desire and guilt ('I feel like a detective spying'). The other came in two poems called 'Babbles', when the lovers were reduced to muttering meaningless phrases that said quite a lot about the inarticulacy of passion.

Otherwise the evening, for all the use of strobe-lighting and a lamp shone in someone's face to denote savagery, struck me as untheatrical and far less informative about the real gut-wrenching quality of desire than any five minutes of Mr. Shepard's astonishing recent play, *Fool for Love*.

Michael Billington, *The Guardian*, 1 May 1984

See also:

Eileen Blumenthal, 'Sam Shepard and Joseph Chaikin: Speaking in Tongues', in *American Dreams*, p. 136-47.

Ellen Oumano, *Sam Shepard* (London: Virgin, 1987), p. 125-9 (interviews with musicians).

James Leverett, 'Other Voices, Other Ruins', *Soho Weekly News*, 22 Nov. 1979, p. 47.

Mel Gussow, 'Intimate Monologues That Speak to the Heart and Mind', *New York Times*, 9 Dec. 1979, Sec. 2, p. 3, 36.

Introductions to *Tongues*, by Shepard, and *Savage/Love*, by Chaikin, in *Seven Plays*.

Jacaranda

Text for dance piece by Daniel Nagrin.
First production: St. Clements Church, New York, 7 June 1979.
Unpublished.

In Jacaranda a man wakes up in his lover's 'rather extravagant' bed. She's not there.

Jennifer Dunning, 'A Nagrin Dance to a Shepard Libretto', *New York Times*, 31 May 1979, Sec. C, p. 13

My work is not written in granite. It's like playing a piece of music. It goes out into the air and dissolves forever.

Shepard, letter to Nagrin

True West

Two-act play.
First production: Magic Th., San Francisco, 10 July 1980 (dir. Robert Woodruff).

First New York production: New York Shakespeare Festival, Public Th., 23 Dec. 1980 (dir. Joseph Papp, replacing Woodruff after dispute).
Revived: Steppenwolf Th., Chicago, 1982, transferring to Cherry Lane Th., New York, 17 Oct. 1982 (dir. Gary Sinise; with Sinise as Austin, John Malkovich as Lee; a film of this production was shown on PBS Television, Jan. 1984).
First London production: Cottesloe Th., London, 10 Dec. 1981 (dir. John Schlesinger; with Antony Sher as Austin, Bob Hoskins as Lee).

Clean-cut screenwriter Austin is holed up at his mother's house in Southern California (she's on vacation in Alaska), finishing a project he's pitching to a Hollywood producer. He is being distracted by his older brother Lee, a slovenly drifter and cat burglar who takes after his father, now living 'out on the desert' , drunk and broke. While the producer meets with Austin, Lee butts in, claiming that he has a good idea for a Western. Something happens over a game of golf — you're not sure if Mr. Producer lost a bet or he threatened the guy — and he decides to drop Austin's story and do Lee's. The brothers switch roles, but Lee can't spell, let alone type, and Austin's idea of crime is stealing all the toasters in the neighbourhood. Mom arrives home from Alaska ... takes one look at her ravaged bungalow and her drunken brawling boys and decides to check into a motel. Moonlight settles on the two brothers circling each other in silent, deadly combat.

Don Shewey, 'The True Story of *True West*',
Village Voice, 30 Nov. 1980

I wanted to write a play about double nature, one that wouldn't be symbolic or metaphorical or any of that stuff. I just wanted to give a taste of what it feels like to be two-sided ... I worked harder on this play than anything I've ever written. The play's down to the bone.

Shepard

True West felt like a total improvisation spinning off itself. The writing of the play started when I heard the voice of Lee speaking very clearly, and then I heard Austin's response. The more I listened, the more the voices came.

Shepard

The effect is of a transatlantic reworking of Pinter's *Homecoming*, a demonstration of the power of blood-ties to undermine and overwhelm, plunder and destroy even those who fancy themselves collected and mature. Today you may be doing very nicely thank you. Tomorrow your brother may materialize from nowhere, and have you inexplicably and hopelessly under his still-capacious thumb.

Yet, Shepard being Shepard, that isn't all there is to the play. Maybe the clue to its subterranean workings comes when the producer remarks that the brothers are 'the same person'. Since Hoskins is a sweaty, lumbering semi-illiterate who yearns only to return to the outback and lay his grubby shirt on 'fighting dogs' and Sher is a dapper suburbanite most obviously at home behind his desk, this comment is either sensationally obtuse or remarkably acute. And the developing evidence tends to support the second theory. Denied his brother's help, Hoskins settles down to the typewriter, only to end by enmeshing himself in its ribbon and dementedly belabouring the machine itself with a golfclub: at the same time Sher turns ineptly macho, getting spectacularly drunk, breaking into neighbourhood houses and stealing toasters from their kitchens, imploring his unimpressed brother to take him to the tough-guy west, and finally trying to throttle him with the phone-cord.

As the play closes, the two men are circling one another in envy, hatred and (conceivably) love, each knowing the other has something he needs and can't acquire, each of them a half-person hankering to be whole. They are complementary, even symbiotic, yet doomed to remain apart. And what Shepard is presumably dramatizing is a psychological and social schizophrenia characteristic of America and, perhaps, of many other cultures, including our own. On the one hand, the thinker, the 'civilized' man, uneasily aware that his education and status have cost him the loss of deeper, more vital juices, on the other, the man of instinct and impulse, frustrated by his inability to cope adequately in a world that increasingly makes him and his look prehistoric.

Benedict Nightingale, *New Statesman*, 13 Dec. 1981

True West is a worthy descendant of Mr. Shepard's *Curse of the Starving Class* and *Buried Child*. Many of his persistent recent themes are present and accounted for — the spiritual death of the American family, the corruption of the artist by business, the vanishing of the Western wilderness and its promised dream of freedom. If the playwright dramatizes his concerns in fantastic flights of poetic imagery, that imagery always springs directly from the life of the people and drama he has created. Mr. Shepard doesn't graft symbols onto his plays. He's a true artist: his best works are organic creations that cannot be broken down into their constituent parts.

Frank Rich, *New York Times*, 24 Dec. 1980, Sec. C, p. 9

See also:

Robert Brustein, 'Crossed Purposes', *New Republic*, 31 Jan. 1981, p. 21-3.

James Fenton, *Sunday Times*, 13 Dec. 1981, p. 38.

William Kleb, 'Worse than Being Homeless: *True West* and the Divided Self' in *American Dreams*, p. 117-25.

Tucker Orbison, 'Mythic Levels in Shepard's *True West*', *Modern Drama*, XXVII, No. 4 (Dec. 1984), p. 506-19.

Superstitions

Theatre piece based on material that became *Motel Chronicles*.

First production: Intersection Th., San Francisco, 1981 (under pseudonym Walker Hayes; with O-Lan Shepard, music by Catherine Stone).

First New York production: La Mama ETC, in a double bill with *The Sad Lament of Pecos Bill*, Sept. 1983 (dir. Julie Hebert).

Unpublished.

See:

Frank Rich, *New York Times*, 20 Sept. 1983.

Benedict Nightingale, *New York Times*, 25 Sept. 1983.

Fool for Love

Long one-act play.

First production: Magic Th., San Francisco, 8 Feb. 1983 (dir. Shepard; with Ed Harris, Kathy Baker).

First New York production: Circle Repertory Th., 26 May 1983 (details as above).

First London production: Cottesloe Th.,4 Oct. 1984 (dir. Peter Gill; with Ian Charleson, Julie Walters).

Adapted by Shepard into screenplay for film by Robert Altman, 1985 (see 'Non-Dramatic Writings').

Published: Fool for Love and The Sad Lament; *Fool for Love and Other Plays.*

Shepard's play is a love story set in a seedy motel room on the edge of the Mojave desert in California. ... Eddie the stuntman has travelled, as he methodically recalls, 2,480 miles to this Godforsaken spot to find May, his love for fifteen years, and to take her across the plains to Wyoming. May has heard it all before; he has loved her and left her and left her again for nearly half her life. Her new date is overdue. She wants to start afresh. ... But as Shepard's play unfolds, it is clear that Eddie and May are bound in blood and tears to part and reunite violently, tortuously and endlessly. They share the same father, an intolerable fact that they discovered too late, and the old man's ghost sits in the shadows, rocking to and fro, interrupting the action, pleading his case, defending the American way of infidelity, putting the man's view, condemning Eddie to go on leaving for ever.

Ros Asquith, *The Observer*, 7 Oct. 1984, p. 19

I was determined to write some kind of confrontation between a man and a woman, as opposed to just men ... this one is really more about a woman than any play I've ever written, and it's from her point of view pretty much, though a man is in there.

She has a date with a docile muscleman who maintains lawns: he is being vengefully pursued by a woman in a black Mercedes Benz. And as we watch Eddie and May tearing each other apart with erotic frenzy under the vigilant eye of an Old Man, we come to realize they are bound together by blood as well as by lust and that their fatal connection can never be totally dissolved.

It is a play one responds to emotionally rather than analytically: Shepard is offering a fragment of a dream rather than a thesis-drama. But to me the work speaks eloquently about the destructive obsessiveness of love (it is packed with images of quest and pursuit of the loved ones), about male notions of ownership, about a specifically American inability to face reality and about the translation of a wild landscape into a world of vegetable gardens and miniature golf-courses. On a personal level, it is a powerful Strindbergian demonstration of the kinship between desire and violence, but deep down it is about our inability to understand our own feelings (there is a poignant moment when May, having brutally rejected Eddie, breaks down in his absence) and about a very American predilection for fantasy symbolized by the

Old Man's rapturous gaze at a non-existent picture of the woman of his dreams. ...

Julie Walters, physically striking in scarlet, is very good at the pillow-clutching pain of love and at one astonishing moment crawls across the floor in self-abasement of desire. Ian Charleson also subtly suggests that under the displaced cowboy who lassoes the bed-posts as a mark of frustration and who hurls himself horizontally against a door to prevent someone passing through there is a sensitive man almost ashamed of his finer feelings. The two actors do everything that could reasonably be expected in terms of self-laceration; but I still feel the play requires an element of reflex physicality that lies beyond our culture.

Michael Billington, *The Guardian*, 5 Oct. 1984

In New York, I found Sam Shepard's *Fool for Love* a strange, bewitching, shattering, dead-of-night sort of play. The author had directed it. Above all, I recall the physical energy of Eddie and May, angels with dirty faces, locked in a sibling impasse of incestuous recriminations, throwing each other hard against the green slimy walls of a motel on the edge of the Mojave desert.

In the National's studio theatre we do not have quite the same thing. We have, to be sure, two outstanding actors, Julie Walters and Ian Charleson, as the sister and half-brother. But the realism is all wrong. This is, under Peter Gill's scrupulous scrubbed direction, a competent display of inflected British acting. But it is not raw, it is not foul, it is not passionate and it is not powerful.

Michael Coveney, *Financial Times*, 5 Oct. 1984

See also:

Bernard Weiner, 'Shepard: Waiting for a Western', *San Francisco Chronicle*, 9 Feb. 1983, p. 54-5 (interview).

Michiko Kakutani, 'Myths, Dreams, Realities — Sam Shepard's America', *New York Times*, 29 Jan. 1984, Sec. 2, p. 1, 26 (interview).

Frank Rich, 'Stage: Fool for Love', *New York Times*, 27 May 1983, Sec. C, p. 3.

Robert Brustein, *New Republic*, 27 June 1983, p. 24-5.

The War in Heaven

Monologue for radio, written with Joseph Chaikin.
First production: WBAI Radio, New York, 8 Jan. 1985 (performed by Chaikin; with music by Shepard).

First London production: Th. Upstairs, Oct. 1987 (with Joseph Chaikin).
Published: A Lie of the Mind and The War in Heaven.

A piece about an angel trapped between two dimensions ... an exquisitely felt poem, reminiscent of Milton's Paradise Lost, *about all of us — trapped angels who scarcely recall their origins — all the more moving when one considers the circumstances under which it was created: Chaikin had difficulty speaking [after a stroke], so Shepard sat many hours by his bed, carefully questioning him and taking notes, painstakingly working through the piece until it was complete.*

Ellen Oumano, *Sam Shepard* (London: Virgin, 1987), p. 150

A Lie of the Mind

Three-act play.

First production: Promenade Th., New York, 5 Dec. 1985 (dir. Shepard; with Harvey Keitel as Jake, Amanda Plummer as Beth, Aidan Quinn as Frankie, Geraldine Page as Lorraine, Will Patton as Mike; music by Red Clay Ramblers).

First London production; Royal Court, 14 Oct. 1987 (dir. Simon Curtis; with Will Patton as Jake, Miranda Richardson as Beth, Paul McGann as Frankie, Geraldine McEwan as Lorraine, Paul Jesson as Mike; music by Stephen Warbeck).

Published: A Lie of the Mind and The War in Heaven; A Lie of the Mind (London: Methuen, 1987).

Two families, occupying separate areas of the stage, are linked by the marriage of Jake and Beth. The play opens with Jake telling his brother Frankie that he has murdered Beth in a jealous rage; in fact she is in Montana, damaged in mind and body, and being cared for by her brother Mike and her father and mother. While Jake seeks sanctuary in his boyhood bed, tended by his mother Lorraine, Frankie travels to the snows of Montana to discover what really happened to Beth. When he reaches the house he is mistaken for a deer and shot in the leg; forced thus to remain there, he becomes close to her. After a symbolic confrontation with the memory of his dead father, an

Air Force pilot, Jake makes the same journey, draped in an American flag. Broken but redeemed, he surrenders Beth to Frankie. The play ends in a scene of reconciliation, with Beth's mother glimpsing 'a fire in the snow'.

That's twenty one years work there. It was a tough play to write, because I had the first act very clearly in mind, then went off on a tangent and had to throw away two acts and start again. Then it began to tell itself. Like a story you've heard a long time ago that's now come back. ... [The starting point was] the incredible schism between a man and a woman, in which something is broken in a way that almost kills the thing that was causing them to be together.

Shepard

The play's most powerful reverberations ... are prompted by those pure Shepard inventions that deliver the evening's inseparable poetry, action and content. It's the one shimmering constant in this work that characters are mistaking the living for the dead, one brother for another brother, sons for fathers, sisters for wives — even, at one loony point, a man for a deer. ... Such repeated confusions ... create a cumulative dramatic sensation not quite like that produced by any other American playwright. We feel we are passing through the turbulent magnetic fields of the play's two interlocked families, almost palpably experiencing the knotted blood ties that keep tugging at the characters on stage. These ties, as immutable as a tribal code, also seem to be the lies of the title. It is the roles the characters play in their eternal family scenarios, the mythic stories that are re-enacted ritualistically in generation after generation, that dog Mr. Shepard's people.

Frank Rich, *New York Times*, 6 Dec. 1985

A Lie of the Mind, Shepard's most ambitious and accessible play to date, may, with any luck, be the grand finale of the so called 'family plays', patently biographical and relatively naturalistic works which start with *Curse of the Starving Class* (1977) and *Buried Child* (1978). ... After the waning of the counter-culture, Shepard's busted kaleidoscope vision of America settled into a quasi-conservative mythic realism. The rhapsodic arias of the earlier work gave way in the family plays to deliberately commonplace, staccato utterances. The primordial struggles of archetypal antagonists were abandoned for biographical quests for identity via family ritual. ... Now Shepard reclaims his landscape, the 'true' West where he was raised, and peoples it with transients ... flakey, abstracted women; absented if not actually absent men — their doomed, dreaming daughters and embattled sons.

Christina Monet, *The Literary Review*, Mar. 1986, p. 25-6

In this play Shepard heaves in all the themes of his recent work: love, the bad seed or dynastic 'curse', the unwilling, martyred paterfamilias, his splintered wife, warring siblings — and he sets it all down in the sort of intellectually barren, mock-heroic prairie-desert towns that grew up when someone's ancestor first threw his horse's halter around a stump. In fact, there are too many themes here.

I first saw the play two years ago in New York: directed by Shepard with the self-regarding Harvey Keitel and Amanda Plummer as lovers who exerted no visible pull on one another or, indeed, on us, it failed for me (though not for the New York critics). Simon Curtis's London production is steadier and less indulgent: it allows the tropism of the two lovers — with Miranda Richardson giving a quite extraordinarily true performance — to drive the play forward. It exacts measured treatment by Deborah Norton and Tony Haygarth as Beth's invincibly loopy parents; and all of the characteristically black yet loving humour that one recognizes as Shepard's province.

There are moments of terrific poignancy when the characters go into arias which describe those subjective sensations which we never otherwise hear about but can all recognize and which is one of Shepard's special gifts. There are also a host of symbols, up to and including no less than the American flag that Jake winds round himself — you can also see shades of *Hamlet* and *The Seagull* if you're so inclined — that lend the play a certain specious weightiness or public feeling which may have also accounted for its good critical reception over there. Ultimately it is a bit too knowing, fuller but also considerably more diagrammatic than Shepard's other recent works. Yet, like them, it continues to rumble in the brain, urging one into private mythopoeia.

Victoria Radin, *New Statesman*, 30 Oct. 1987

Sam Shepard's *A Lie of The Mind* is as strange and haunting a play as you will find in London. It is like a three-act ballad abut Oedipal myths, the bizarre nature of love, the craziness of Middle America. But its meaning emerges more through its mood than through any direct statement; and that mood is beautifully captured in Simon Curtis's Royal Court production which has far more lyricism than the one by Shepard himself I saw in New York last year. ...

Shepard's most striking qualities ... are his charity and humour. He writes uncensoriously about the weirdest people and reveals the absurdity of the everyday. Jake's mother, for instance, keeps her husband's ashes under a bed and remarks, with the utmost casualness, 'He's a lot lighter than he was.'

And Beth's twilit mother who believes she was once locked up in hospital is reminded none too gently by her husband, 'That wasn't you, that was your mother.' As Shepard's title implies, these people all live inside their own heads where the light of reality rarely penetrates.

Simon Curtis craftily extends Shepard's device of putting a blue-grass trio on stage to underscore the action and give the play a more plangent quality than it had in New York. Paul Brown's set, with its abandoned North Dakota automobile and its motor-radiator motifs, also exudes the right atmosphere of decaying Americana. And, though the accents wobble, the acting is often spectacularly good.

Michael Billington, *The Guardian*, 22 Oct. 1987

Marvellous at every stage, Miranda Richardson first shows you Beth as a bandaged casualty tottering her way back towards movement and speech, then as a half-amnesiac creature, and finally as an over-made-up eyelash-batting bobby-soxer. This metamorphosis — from calamity to caricature — typifies Shepard's style. He takes episodes of family fraughtness that could have come from O'Neill and gives them the bouncy artificiality of a cartoon strip. Blows fall, guns blast, members of feuding families are trapped together in a blizzard, but no lasting harm is done. Injuries knit, partners unite, traumas are healthily shed.

Jake's assault on Beth, the play fondly intimates, springs from violent love. Deep down, she knows this. Ultimately demonstrating how much he cares, he benevolently releases her towards a gentler mate, his brother, Frankie. Resembling Jake, but lacking his aggression, Frankie — nicely played by Paul McGann — personifies the play's ideal: a balanced blending of qualities from those 'two opposite animals', male and female.

Peter Kemp, *The Independent*, 22 Oct. 1987

See also:

Blanche McCrary Boyd, 'The Natural', *American Film*, Oct. 1984, p. 22-6, 91-2 (interview).

Samuel Freedman, 'Sam Shepard's Mythic Vision of the Family', *New York Times*, 1 Dec. 1985, Sec. 2, p. 1, 20.

Jonathan Cott, 'The Rolling Stone Interview: Sam Shepard', *Rolling Stone*, 18 Dec. 1986, p. 166, 168 170, 172, 198, 200.

Nan Robertson, 'The Multidimensional Sam Shepard', *New York Times*, 21 Jan. 1986, Sec C, p. 15.

b: Group Collaboration

Nightwalk

'Collective work', with Jean-Claude van Itallie and Megan Terry.
First production: Open Th., St. Clement's Church, New York,
     8 Sept. 1973.
First London production: by the Open Th., Round House, June 1973.
Unpublished.

The absurdist element, evident in [the Open Theatre's] earlier plays,
exists equally in this last work as God is indicted for his absence and the
consequent sense of absurdity is compounded by the materialism and
sexual role-playing of society. But the play is part satire, part
celebration. The same characters who enact the grotesques of the social
world also perform the physical arabesques which imply a level of lyric
potential. There is a struggle for supremacy, resolved in the direction of
wholeness. The move seems to be in the direction of celebration. But the
play was incomplete — a work in progress which was never further
refined because of the disbandment of the group.

C.W.E. Bigsby,
A Critical Introduction to Twentieth-Century American Drama,Vol. 3:
Beyond Broadway, p. 121

a: Film Scripts

Unfilmed screenplays include *Maxagasm* (for the Rolling Stones), *Ringaleerio*, and *Bodyguard* (from *The Changeling*).

Me and My Brother

Dir. Robert Frank; with Julius and Peter Orlovsky, Joe Chaikin.
Released: 1968. Uncredited contributions to dialogue by Shepard.

Zabriskie Point

Dir. Michelangelo Antonioni; with Mark Frechette, Daria Halpern.
Released: 1970. Screenplay is credited to Antonioni, Tonino Guerra, Fred Gardner, Clare Peploe, and Shepard.

Paris, Texas

Dir. Wim Wenders; with Harry Dean Stanton, Nastassia Kinski.
Released: 1984. An illustrated text based on the finished film, explicitly 'not the screenplay as it was written by Sam Shepard before the film went into shooting', was published, ed. Chris Sievernich (Greno: Road Movies, 1984; New York: Norton, for Ecco, 1985).

Fool for Love

Adapted from the stage play. Dir. Robert Altman; with Kim Basinger, Harry Dean Stanton, and Shepard.
Released: 1985

Far North

Dir. Shepard; with Jessica Lange, Charles Durning, Ann Wedgeworth, Tess Harper, Donald Moffatt, Nina Draxten.
Released: 1988.

b: Other Writings

Hawk Moon

Los Angeles: Black Sparrow Press, 1973; New York: Performing Arts Journal Publications, 1981. 'A book of short stories, poems, and monologues.'

Rolling Thunder Logbook

New York: Viking Press, 1977. London: Penguin, 1978. Diary of Bob Dylan's 'Rolling Thunder Revue' tour in 1975.

Motel Chronicles

San Francisco: City Lights Books, 1982. Mixture of journal entries, poems and memories. Published with *Hawk Moon*, London: Faber, 1985.

c: Song

Lyric of 'Brownsville Girl', co-written with Bob Dylan, for his album *Knocked Out Loaded*, 1986.

'Originality from Ignorance'

I hardly knew anything about the theatre. I remember once in California I went to this guy's house who was called a beatnik by everybody in the school because he had a beard and he wore sandals. And we were listening to some jazz or something and he sort of shuffled over to me and threw this book on my lap and said, why don't you dig this, you know. I started reading this play he gave me, and it was like nothing I'd ever read before — it was *Waiting for Godot*. And I thought, what's this guy talking about, what is this? And I read it with a very keen interest, but I didn't know anything about what it *was*. I didn't really have any references for the theatre, except for the few plays that I'd acted in. But in a way I think that was better for me, because I didn't have any idea about how to shape an action into what is seen — so the so-called originality of the early work just comes from ignorance. I just didn't know.

Interview in *Theatre Quarterly*, p. 5

New York in the Early 'Sixties

On the Lower East Side there *was* a special sort of culture developing. You were so close to the people who were going to the plays, there was really no difference between you and them — your own experience was their experience, so that you began to develop that consciousness of what was happening. ... I mean nobody knew what *was* happening, but there was a sense that something was going on. People were arriving from Texas and Arkansas in the middle of New York City, and a community was being established. It was a very exciting time. ...

I was very lucky to have arrived in New York at that time, though, because the whole off-off-Broadway theatre was just starting — like Ellen Stewart with her little cafe, and Joe Cino, and the Judson Poets Theatre and all these places. It was just a lucky accident really that I arrived at the same time as that was all starting. This was before they had all become famous, of course — like Ellen just had this little loft, served hot chocolate and coffee, did these plays.

Interview in *Theatre Quarterly*, p. 6-8

Looking Back at the Early Work

Things used to *attack* me in the mind. I had no idea where they were coming from, or why they were there, and I used to get more and more fascinated and look at them and mess around ... and it turns out it's a waste of time. There's a much more creative life to the mind than following all the *junk*. Anybody can be destructive. For a long time I don't think I understood the nature of the mind, how the mind actually works. So a lot of those things aren't even worth looking into. It's just, they're like devils. You're causing yourself more trouble. If you start indulging in thought forms that are destructive.

> Interviewed by Jennifer Allen, *Esquire*, Nov. 1988, p. 148

Secrets and Added Dimensions

Every play is a discovery. You create a framework ... and leave something open in the hope you will discover something. Whether it has a name to it I don't know, but with a really great writer like Samuel Beckett, every time he writes he is approaching a certain kind of secret. As he approaches it the audience is approaching it too. As soon as you name it you kill it. There is no question of naming and having it at the same time.

> Interviewed by Michael White, 'Underground Landscapes',
> *The Guardian*, 20 Feb. 1974, p. 8

The fantastic thing about theatre is that it can make something be seen that's invisible, and that's where my interest in theatre is — that you can be watching this thing happening with actors and costumes and light and set and language, and even plot, and something emerges from beyond that, and that's the image part that I'm looking for, that's the sort of added dimension.

> Interview in *Theatre Quarterly*, p. 9

On Emotion and Myth

In writing a play you can snare emotions that aren't just personal emotions, not just catharsis, not just psychological emotions that you're getting off your chest, but emotions and feelings that are connected with everybody. Hopefully. It's not true all the time; sometimes it's nothing but self-indulgence. But if you work hard enough toward being true to what you intuitively feel is going down in the play, you might be able to catch that kind of thing. So that you suddenly hook up with feelings that are on a very broad scale ... you start with something personal and see how it follows out and opens to something that's much bigger. ... Then it starts to move in a direction we all know, regardless of where we come from or who we are. It starts to hook up in a certain way. Those, to me, are mythic emotions.

Interviewed by Amy Lippman,
Dialogue, Apr. 1985, p. 58

Jazz and Other Music

Jazz could move in surprising territory without qualifying itself. You could follow a traditional melody and then break away, and then come back, or drop into polyrhythms. You could have three, four things going on simultaneously. But, more importantly, it was an emotional thing. You could move in all these emotional territories, and you could do it with *passion*. You could throw yourself into a passage, and then you could calm down, then you could ride this thing, then you could throw yourself *in* again. ... I felt this urban thing was what was really happening. Jazz was what I wanted to dive into; it represented a kind of sophistication. Then after a while I started reacting against that, the whole jazz influence. So I began to think rock and roll music represented another kind of back to a raw gut kind of American shit-kicker thing. Then that came to an end. Now I'm back to country music.

Interviewed by Pete Hamill, 'The New American Hero',
New York, 5 Dec. 1983, p. 80

One-Act Form, Audiences, and the Cultural Machine

Because of the time we're living in, the attention span of people watching a work has changed. It's no longer possible for an audience to sit alertly through *Long Day's Journey into Night*, even though it's a great play in the sense that it's part of an American tradition of theatre. But to me, it's more interesting to condense time into something that's full and yet short enough so that people will be with it, can stay with it, in a certain way. Beckett, for instance, has shortened and condensed everything down to its most essential parts, which I think is amazing. And still, Beckett's plays are considered great works — which has probably never happened before — that a man can write a five-minute

57

piece which is considered a great play. Before, the attitude always was that you had to write fourteen-act operas and all that shit.

Interviewed by Irene Oppenheim and Victor Fascio,
Village Voice, 27 Oct. 1975, p. 82

In the realm of experimental writing for the theatre, a young writer is gradually persuaded that the 'one-act' form is a stepping stone toward the creation of 'full-length' plays and that, finally, when he begins to grind out these monsters they alone can serve as proof of his literary value to the public. The term 'full-length' has for a long time been synonymous with a play of two acts or more and has relegated shorter works to the status of 'experimentation'. The cultural machine that encourages young writers to experiment, in the same breath encourages them to quickly grow out of it and start producing 'major works'. ...

My concern is mainly with the playwright and his personal sense of time in relationship to his work. How that sense of time is correlated between his work on paper and its appearance in three dimensions. And finally how that sense of time becomes squeezed and pulled into conventional lengths for the viewing public. Writers are still under the influence of producers, critics, agents, etc., who demand that the real value of a piece of work has to be gleaned from its content only and that the total experience of the piece (including its length) is something set apart and even something that can be 'doctored up' to suit the needs of the individual theatre and its audience.

Another part of this syndrome is the difficulty a playwright has in returning to attempts at shorter works after having 'accomplished' one or two longer plays. The demand from the outside is always for the next 'full-length, major opus' and anything shorter can only be taken as either some regression or an intermediary to something bigger. Rarely is it seen for what it is — a part of the gradually unfolding process of a playwright's total work.

Interviewed in *American Place Theatre Newsletter*, 1975

On Stories

The stories my characters tell are stories that are always unfinished, always imagistic — having to do with recalling experiences through a certain kind of vision. They're always fractured and fragmented and broken. I'd love to be able to tell a classic story, but it doesn't seem to be part of my nature.

Interviewed by Michiko Kakutani,
New York Times, 29 Jan. 1984, Sec. 2, p. 26

Changing Direction

I'd been writing for ten years in an experimental maze — poking around, fishing in the dark. I wasn't going anywhere. I felt I needed an aim in the work versus just the instinctive stuff, which is very easy for me to do. I started with character, in all its complexities. As I got more and more into it, it led me to the family. I always did feel a part of that tradition but *hated* it. I couldn't stand those plays that were all about the 'turmoil' of the family. And then all of a sudden I realized, well that was very much a part of my life, and maybe that has to do with being a playwright, that you're somehow snared beyond yourself.

Interviewed by Jennifer Allen, as above, p. 148

On Character

[The evolution in the work] has to do with moving inside the character. Originally, I was fascinated by form, by exteriors — starting from the outside and going in, with the idea that character is something shifting and that it can shift from one person to another. You had different attitudes drifting in and out from actors who are part of the ensemble. So in the past, it was the overall tone of the piece I was interested in rather than in characters as individuals. That sort of played itself out, and for a while I didn't know where to go from there. But then I started to delve into character.

Interviewed by Michiko Kakutani, as above

From Arias to Simplicity

One of the things I've found is that it's too much to expect an actor to do a vocal aria, standing there in the middle of the stage and have the thing work in space, without actually having him physically involved in what he's talking about. The speeches have been shaved quite considerably since the early plays, I don't go in for long speeches any more.

Interview in *Theatre Quarterly*, p. 14

I think you have to start in colloquial territory, and from there move on and arrive in poetic country ... but not the other way around. I've noticed that even with the Greek guys, especially with Sophocles, there's a very simple, rawboned language. The choruses are poetic, but the speech of the characters themselves is terse, cut to the bone and pointed to the heart of the problem.

Interviewed by Jonathan Cott, *Rolling Stone,* 18 Dec. 1986, p. 170

On Endings

I think it's a cheap trick to resolve things. It's totally a complete lie to make resolutions: I've always felt that, particularly in the theatre when everything's tied up at the end with a neat little ribbon and you're delivered this package. You walk out of the theatre feeling that everything's resolved and you know what the play's all about. So what? It's almost as though why go through all that if you're just going to tie it all up at the end? It seems like a lie to me — the resolutions, the denouement and all the rest of it. And it's been handed down as if that is the way to write plays. ... I never know when to end a play. I'd just as soon not end anything. But you have to stop at some point, just to let people out of the theatre. I don't like endings and I have a hard time with them. So *True West* doesn't really have an ending; it has a confrontation. A resolution isn't an ending; it's a strangulation.

Interviewed by Amy Lippman, as above, p. 59

On Broadway

My reservations about Broadway go beyond the 'commercialism' stigma. I really believe the theatre is an experience of intimacy, a personal transaction between actors and audience. As the audience increases in size, the intimacy is reduced and becomes absorbed in a kind of mass psychology. Reactions sweep through the audience overtaking the individual and causing him to believe they're his own reactions. Sometimes this sensation may be thrilling but it often has little to do with, and often robs the person of, the experience.

Letter to author in Doris Auerbach,
Sam Shepard, Arthur Kopit and the Off-Broadway Theatre,
(Boston: Twayne, 1982), p. 53-4

On O'Neill

Plays have to go beyond just 'working out problems'. ... What makes O'Neill's *Long Day's Journey into Night* such a great work, for instance, is that O'Neill moves past his own personal family situation into a much wider dimension. I read that play in high school, and I've always thought that that was truly the great American play. It's so overwhelmingly honest — O'Neill just doesn't pull any punches. You can't confront that play without being moved.

Interviewed by Jonathan Cott, as above, p. 172

On Brecht

With Brecht, I think his attraction for me was his 'tough guy' stance in the midst of the intellectual circle of his times. His embracing aspects of the American subculture (Chicago gangsters, Alaskan opportunists, etc.). His fascination with boxing, befriending a heavyweight of the era, writing and singing songs on his guitar, his poetry, his theory, his direct involvement with actors and the problem of meeting the audience face to face with the theatrical event. His understanding of the fact of duality and that every coin has two sides. His ability to find the perfect collaboration with Kurt Weill. In other words, his voracious appetite for the life around him and his continuous adaptability to search out a true expression and put it into practice. His concern was for a total theatre but one stripped to the bare necessity.

Letter to author in Doris Auerbach, as above, p. 30

On Directing

I like to start from zero. From absolutely nothing. Every actor has a different method of approach, depending on his school, depending on his experience, all that stuff. So you have to, right from the beginning, accept the fact that everybody's going to be working subjectively in a different way. So the task of the director seems to me how to pull everybody into one territory of equality and also allow them to go ahead and work individually. And the equality seems to be the body because everybody knows, more or less, the functions that are involved in the sensory experiences. So if you take that as a first base, everybody's connected on that level and starts to work just strictly from the physical body and how it has to find its way into the character. Then everybody begins to work on similar levels. And you allow all the rest of it to go on. I mean, if somebody wants to work by Lee Strasberg's method or Stanislavski or something else, you allow all that, so long as everybody's connected with this idea that the sensory experience is the essential. In other words, how does a character smell, taste, see, hear, and feel? And then from there you have a ground for it.

Interviewed by Ross Wetzsteon, *Village Voice*, 10 Dec. 1985, p. 56

On the Theatre of the Absurd

It was a movement that more or less coincided with off-Broadway but it remained European in its psychological stance. I felt it was important that an American playwright speak with an American tongue, not only in a vernacular sense, but that he should inhabit the stage with American being. The American playwright should snarl and spit, not whimper and whine.

As above, p. 41

On Machismo and Violence

Just because machismo exists doesn't mean that it shouldn't exist. There's this attitude today that certain antagonistic forces have to be ignored or completely shut out rather than entered into in order to explore and get to the heart of them. ... So rather than avoid the issue, why not take a dive into it? I'm not saying whether it's good or bad — I think that the moralistic approach to these notions is stupid. It's not a moral issue, it's an issue of existence. Machismo may be an evil force ... but what in fact is it? ... I know what this thing is about because I was a victim of it, it was part of my life, my old man tried to force on me a notion of what it was to be a 'man'. And it destroyed my dad. But you can't avoid facing it.

Interviewed by Jonathan Cott, as above, p. 172

I think there's something about American violence that to me is very touching. In full force it's very ugly, but there's also something very moving about it, because it has to do with humiliation. There's some hidden, deeply-rooted thing in the Anglo male American that has to do with inferiority, that has to do with not being a man, and always, continually having to act out some idea of manhood that invariably is violent. This sense of failure runs very deep — maybe it has to do with the frontier being systematically taken away, with the guilt of having gotten this country by wiping out a native race of people, with the whole Protestant work ethic. I can't put my finger on it, but it's the source of a lot of intrigue for me.

Interviewed by Michiko Kakutani, as above, p. 26

On the American West

I just feel like the West is much more ancient than the East. ... There are areas like Wyoming, Texas, Montana and places like that, where you really feel this ancient thing about the land. Ancient. That it's primordial ... It has to do with the relationship between the land and the people — between the human being and the ground. I think that's typically western and much more attractive than this tight little forest civilization that happened back East. It's much more physical and emotional to me. New England and the East Coast have always been an intellectual community. ... I just feel like I'll never get over the fact of being from the West.

Interviewed by Amy Lippman, as above, p. 59

On Parasites

Once, in New Mexico, I observed these incredibly beautiful red-tailed hawks — with a wing-span of five feet — which started out gliding in these arroyos way down low. And these crows come and bother them — they're after fleas and peck at the hawks and drive them nuts, because they're looking for something else. And I watched a crow diving at and bothering this one hawk, which just flew higher and higher until it was so far up that the crow couldn't follow it anymore and had to come back down.

So the answer is to outfly them.

Yeah, outfly them. Avoid situations that are going to take pieces of you. And hide out.

Interviewed by Jonathan Cott, as above, p. 200

a: Primary Sources

Collections of Plays

Publication details of individual plays may be found under their titles in Section 2.

Five Plays. Indianapolis: Bobbs-Merrill, 1967; London: Faber, 1969. [*Chicago, Icarus's Mother, Fourteen Hundred Thousand, Red Cross, Melodrama Play*.]

The Unseen Hand and Other Plays. Indianapolis: Bobbs-Merrill, 1971. [*The Unseen Hand, 4-H Club, Shaved Splits, Forensic and the Navigators, The Holy Ghostly, Back Bog Beast Bait*.]

Mad Dog Blues and Other Plays. New York: Winter House, 1972. [*Rock Garden, Mad Dog Blues, Cowboys No. 2, Cowboy Mouth, Blue Bitch, Nightwalk*.]

The Tooth of Crime and Geography of a Horse Dreamer. New York: Grove Press, 1974.

Action and The Unseen Hand. London: Faber, 1975.

Angel City, Curse of the Starving Class, and Other Plays, with an Introduction by Jack Gelber. New York: Urizen Books, 1976; London: Faber, 1978 (as *Angel City and Other Plays*). [*Angel City, Curse of the Starving Class, Killer's Head, Action, Mad Dog Blues, Cowboy Mouth, Rock Garden, Cowboys No. 2*.]

Buried Child and Seduced and Suicide in B^b. New York: Urizen Books, 1979; London: Faber, 1980.

Seven Plays, with an Introduction by Richard Gilman. New York: Bantam, 1981; London: Faber, 1985. [*Buried Child, Curse of the Starving Class, The Tooth of Crime, La Turista, True West, Tongues, Savage/Love*.]

Four Two-Act Plays. New York: Urizen Books, 1981; London: Faber, 1981. [*La Turista, The Tooth of Crime, Geography of a Horse Dreamer, Operation Sidewinder*.]

Chicago and Other Plays. New York: Urizen Books, 1981; London: Faber, 1982. [Retitled reissue of *Five Plays*.]

Fool for Love and The Sad Lament of Pecos Bill on the Eve of Killing his Wife. San Francisco: City Lights, 1983; London: Faber, 1984.

Fool for Love and Other Plays, with an Introduction by Ross Wetzsteon. New York: Bantam, 1984. [*Angel City, Geography of a Horse Dreamer, Action, Cowboy Mouth,*

Melodrama Play, Seduced, Suicide in B♭.]
The Unseen Hand and Other Plays, with an Introduction by Shepard.
New York: Bantam, 1986. [The Unseen Hand, Rock Garden,
Chicago, Icarus's Mother, 4-H Club, Fourteen Hundred Thousand,
Red Cross, Cowboys No. 2, Forensic and the Navigators, The Holy
Ghostly, Operation Sidewinder, Mad Dog Blues, Back Bog Beast
Bait, Killer's Head.]
A Lie of the Mind and The War in Heaven. New York: New American
Library, 1987.
A Lie of the Mind. London: Methuen, 1987.

Articles and Other Short Prose Pieces

'Autobiography', News of the American Place Theatre, Apr. 1971.
'News Blues', Time Out, No. 222, 31 May-6 June 1974, p. 17. [Piece
wondering 'what kind of significance a play can have' in the face of
the news, on the eve of the Royal Court production of The Tooth of
Crime.]
'Less Than Half a Minute', Time Out, No. 228, 12-18 July 1974,
p. 16-17. [On greyhound racing.]
'Time', American Place Theatre Newsletter, 1975; reprinted in
American Dreams. [On the pressure to write 'full-length' work, when
the writer's true need may be to 'strip everything down to the bones
and start over'.]
'American Experimental Theatre Then and Now', Performing Arts
Journal, II, No. 2 (Fall 1977); reprinted in American Dreams.
[Also brief; the only important residue of the 'sixties is 'the idea of
consciousness'.]
'Language, Visualization and the Inner Library', Drama Review,
XXI, No. 4 (Dec. 1977); reprinted in American Dreams. [On images,
words, myth, and the 'real quest' to penetrate into 'a world behind the
form', rejecting the assumption that plays are about ideas.]
'Introduction' to The Unseen Hand and Other Plays (New York:
Bantam, 1986). [Only a page: on the off-off-Broadway theatre for
which these early plays were written.]

Interviews

Mel Gussow, 'Sam Shepard: Writer on the Way Up', New York Times,
12 Nov. 1969, p. 42.
Naseem Khan, 'Free Form Playwright', Time Out, 7-13 July 1972,
p. 30-1.
Michael White, 'Underground Landscapes', The Guardian,
20 Feb. 1974, p. 8.

Kenneth Chubb and the Editors of *Theatre Quarterly*, 'Metaphors, Mad Dogs and Old Time Cowboys', *Theatre Quarterly*, IV, No. 15 (Aug.-Oct. 1974), p. 3-16. Reprinted in Bonnie Marranca, ed. *American Dreams: the Imagination of Sam Shepard* (New York: Performing Arts Journal, 1981), p. 187-209.

Irene Oppenheim, Victor Fascio, 'The Most Promising Playwright in America Today is Sam Shepard', *Village Voice*, 27 Oct. 1975, p. 81-2.

Roger Downey, 'Inside the Words', *Time Out*, 22-28 Apr. 1977, p. 11.

Michael Vermeulen, 'Sam Shepard: Yes Yes Yes', *Esquire,* Feb. 1980, p. 79-86.

David Ansen, 'The Reluctant Star', *Newsweek*, 17 Nov. 1980, p. 117-18.

Robert Coe, 'Saga of Sam Shepard', *New York Times Magazine*, 23 Nov. 1980, p. 56, 58, 118, 120, 124.

Stewart McBride, 'Sam Shepard', *Christian Science Monitor*, 23 Dec. 1980, Sec. B, p. 2-3.

Ann McFerran, 'Poet of Post-War Americana', *Time Out*, 4-10 Dec. 1981, p. 24-5.

Bernard Weiner, 'Shepard: Waiting for a Western', *San Francisco Chronicle*, 9 Feb. 1983, p. 54-5.

Pete Hamill, 'The New American Hero', *New York*, 5 Dec. 1983, p. 75-6, 78, 80, 84, 86, 88, 90, 92, 95, 96-98, 100, 102.

Pete Hamill, 'Playwright Shepard: On the Set ... and behind the Scenes', *Boston Globe*, 23 Dec. 1983, p. 38-9.

Michiko Kakutani, 'Myths, Dreams, Realities — Sam Shepard's America', *New York Times*, 29 Jan. 1984, Sec. 2, p. 1, 26.

Chris Peachment, 'The Time Out Interview: American Hero', *Time Out*, 23-29 Aug. 1984, p. 14-17.

Stephen Fay, 'Renaissance Man Rides out of the West', *Sunday Times Magazine*, 26 Aug. 1984, p. 16, 19.

Blanche McCrary Boyd, 'The Natural', *American Film*, Oct. 1984, p. 23-6, 91-2. Version appeared as 'True West!' in *The Face*, Mar. 1985, p. 22-6.

Amy Lippman, 'An Interview with Playwright Sam Shepard', *Dialogue*, Apr. 1985, p. 50, 58-9. Reprinted from *Harvard Advocate*, 1983.

Jack Kroll, 'Who's That Tall, Dark Stranger?', *Newsweek*, 11 Nov. 1985.

Ross Wetzsteon, 'Unknown Territory', *Village Voice*, 10 Dec. 1985, p. 55-6.

Jonathan Cott, 'The Rolling Stone Interview: Sam Shepard', *Rolling Stone*, 18 Dec. 1986, p. 166, 168, 170, 172, 198, 200.

Jennifer Allen, 'The Man on the High Horse', *Esquire*, Nov. 1988, p. 141-4, 146, 148, 150-1.

b: Secondary Sources

Full-Length Studies

Bonnie Marranca, ed., *American Dreams: the Imagination of Sam Shepard*. New York: Performing Arts Journal Publications, 1981. [Includes 1974 *Theatre Quarterly* interview, short articles by Shepard, and several critical essays. Elsewhere referred to as *American Dreams*.]

Doris Auerbach, *Sam Shepard, Arthur Kopit and the Off-Broadway Theatre*. Boston: Twayne, 1982.

Ron Mottram, *Inner Landscapes: the Theater of Sam Shepard*. Columbia: University of Missouri Press, 1984.

Don Shewey, *Sam Shepard*. New York: Dell, 1985. [Biography with some criticism.]

Ellen Oumano, *Sam Shepard: the Life and Work of an American Dreamer*. New York: St. Martins Press, 1986; London: Virgin, 1987.

Articles and Chapters in Books

Elizabeth Hardwick, Introduction to *La Turista* (New York: Bobbs-Merrill, 1968). Reprinted as Introduction to *Four Two-Act Plays* (London: Faber, 1981), and in *American Dreams*, p. 67-71.

Ralph Cook, Michael Smith, Sydney Schubert Walter, Jacques Levy, 'Director's Notes', in Shepard, *Five Plays* (London: Faber, 1969).

Ren Frutkin, 'Sam Shepard: Paired Existence Meets the Monster', *Yale/Theatre*, II, 2 (Summer 1969), p. 22-30. Reprinted in *American Dreams*, p. 108-116.

Michael Smith, Introduction to *The Best of Off-Off-Broadway* (New York: Dutton, 1969), p. 9-19.

Gerald Weales, *The Jumping-Off Place: American Drama in the 1960s* (New York: Macmillan, 1969), p. 241-3.

Richard A. Davis, 'Get Up Out a' Your Homemade Beds: the Plays of Sam Shepard', *Players*, XLVII (Oct.-Nov. 1971), p. 12-19.

Albert Poland, Bruce Mailman, *The Off-Off-Broadway Book* (New York: Bobbs-Merrill, 1972).

Michael Smith, Introduction to *More Plays from Off-Off-Broadway* (New York: Bobbs-Merrill, 1972), p. vii-xii.

Charles Marowitz, 'Sam Shepard: Sophisticate Abroad', *Village Voice*, 7 Sept. 1972, p. 52.

John Lahr, 'Jules Feiffer and Sam Shepard: Spectacles of Disintegration', in *Astonish Me* (New York: Viking, 1973), p. 102-19.

Walter Donohue, 'American Graffiti', *Plays and Players*, XXI, 7 (Apr. 1974), p. 14-18.

Kenneth Chubb, 'Fruitful Difficulties of Directing Shepard', *Theatre Quarterly*, IV, No. 15 (Aug.-Oct. 1974), p. 17-25.

Catharine Hughes, *American Playwrights 1945-75* (London: Pitman, 1976), p. 72-80.

Jack Gelber, 'The Playwright as Shaman', Introduction to *Angel City and Other Plays* (San Francisco: Urizen Books, 1976). Reprinted in *American Dreams*, p. 45-8.

Kenneth Chubb, 'Sam Shepard's London', *Canadian Theatre Review*, 10 (Spring 1976), p. 119-22.

Charles R. Bachman, 'Defusion of Meance in the Plays of Sam Shepard', *Modern Drama*, XIX, 4 (Dec. 1976), p. 405-16.

Mel Gussow, 'The Deeply American Roots of Sam Shepard's Plays', *New York Times*, 2 Jan. 1979, Sec. C, p. 7.

Richard Eder, 'Sam Shepard's Obsession is America', *New York Times*, 4 Mar. 1979, Sec. 2, p. 1, 27.

Florence Falk, 'The Role of Performance in Sam Shepard's Plays', *Theatre Journal*, XXXIII, 2 (May 1981), p. 182-98.

Bonnie Marranca, 'Alphabetical Shepard: the Play of Words', *Performing Arts Journal*, V, 2 (1981), p. 9-25. Reprinted in *American Dreams,* p. 13-33.

Gerald Weales, 'The Transformations of Sam Shepard', in *American Dreams*, p. 37-44.

Robert Coe, 'An Interview with Robert Woodruff', in *American Dreams*, p. 151-8.

Robert Coe, 'Image Shots Are Blown: the Rock Plays', in *American Dreams*, p. 57-66.

Michael Bloom, 'Visions of the End: the Early Plays', in *American Dreams*, p. 72-8.

Florence Falk, 'Men Without Women: the Shepard Landscape', in *American Dreams*, p. 90-103.

Joyce Aaron, 'Clues in a Memory', in *American Dreams*, p. 171-4.

Richard Gilman, Introduction to *Seven Plays* (New York: Bantam, 1981). Reprinted in *Seven Plays* (London: Faber, 1985), p. xi-xxvii.

Bonnie Marranca, 'Sam Shepard', in Bonnie Marranca, Gautam Dasgupta, *American Playwrights: a Critical Survey* (New York: Drama Book Specialists, 1981), p. 81-111.

Ruby Cohn, *New American Dramatists 1960-1980* (New York: Grove Press, 1982), p. 171-86.

Ross Wetzsteon, 'Sam Shepard: Escape Artist', *Partisan Review*, XLIX, 2 (1982), p. 253-61.

David Thomson, 'Shepard', *Film Comment*, Nov.-Dec. 1983, p. 49-55.

Herbert Blau, 'The American Dream in American Gothic: the Plays of

Sam Shepard and Adrienne Kennedy', *Modern Drama*, XXVII, 4 (Dec. 1984), p. 520-39.

Robert Wetzsteon, Introduction to *Fool for Love and Other Plays* (New York: Bantam, 1984), p. 1-15.

Eileen Blumenthal, *Joseph Chaikin* (Cambridge: Cambridge University Press, 1984), p. 171-84.

C.W.E. Bigsby, *A Critical Introduction to Twentieth Century American Drama, Vol. 3: Beyond Broadway* (Cambridge: Cambridge University Press, 1985), p. 221-50.

Dennis Carroll, 'The Filmic Cut and "Switchback" in the Plays of Sam Shepard', *Modern Drama*, XXVIII, 1 (Mar. 1985), p. 125-38.

Michael Hoffman, 'Drive, He Said', *TLS*, 1 Mar. 1985, p. 227.

David Jones, 'Sam, Sam, Mythological Man', *London Review of Books*, 2 May 1985, p. 13-14.

Robert Mazzocco, 'Heading for the Last Round Up', *New York Review of Books*, 9 May 1985, p. 21-7.

Samuel G. Freedman, 'Sam Shepard's Mythic Vision of the Family', *New York Times*, 1 Dec. 1985, Sec. 2, p. 1, 20.

Nan Robertson, 'The Multidimensional Sam Shepard', *New York Times*, 21 Jan. 1985, Sec. C, p. 15.

Reference

C.W.E. Bigsby, Kenneth Chubb, and Malcolm Page, 'Theatre Checklist No. 3: Sam Shepard', *Theatrefacts*, No. 3 (Aug.-Oct. 1974), p. 3-11.

'Shepard, Sam', in *Current Biography*, XL, 4 (Apr. 1979), p. 33-7.

'Shepard, Sam', in *Contemporary Authors*, New Revision Series (Detroit: Gale Research Co., 1988), XXII, p. 422-9.